REAL WORLD LITERACY SKILLS

ROBERT A. SNOW

Assistant Superintendent
Somerville, Massachusetts, Public Schools

Author of
Reading Skills and **Advanced Reading Skills**

AMSCO SCHOOL PUBLICATIONS, INC.
315 HUDSON STREET / NEW YORK, N. Y. 10013

As an English and reading teacher at both the secondary and elementary levels in Massachusetts, Robert Snow has taught thousands of students. As well, Mr. Snow has served as department chair, curriculum director, and assistant superintendent in the public school setting. He is also a graduate of the Harvard Graduate School of Education. He has been a guest lecturer at the university level and frequently directs workshops in the New England area for K-12 staff and parents.

Cover and Text Design: Merrill Haber

Unit Opening Photo Credits

Unit 1: FPG
Unit 2: The Stock Market
Unit 3: The Stock Market
Unit 4: The Stock Market
Unit 5: Comstock
Unit 6: The Stock Market
Unit 7: The Stock Market
Unit 8: The Stock Market
Unit 9: The Stock Market
Unit 10: The Stock Market
Unit 11: The Stock Market
Unit 12: The Stock Market
Unit 13: The Stock Market
Unit 14: Comstock
Unit 15: The Stock Market
Unit 16: The Stock Market

Please visit our Web site at:

www.amscopub.com

When ordering this book you may specify: either **R 650 W** or *REAL WORLD LITERACY SKILLS*

ISBN 1-56765-044-9
NYC Item 56765-044-8

Printed in the United States of America

7 8 9 10 11   01 02 03 04 05

This book is dedicated in fond memory of my three good friends, Mr. Donald Brunelli, Jr., Mr. Vernon Eldringhoff, and Mr. Richard Hallett who passed away during production of this book. Their lives and contributions will continue to advance literacy for our families, students, and communities in a variety of ways for many years to come.

TO THE TEACHER

Real World Literacy Skills provides sixteen thematic units to improve reading, writing, organizational, and thinking skills that students need in school and the real world. Specific literacy skills include vocabulary, comprehension, study skills, and sentence and paragraph writing skills after each selection of each unit. Students apply their understanding of these skills through precisely guided questions and activities. At the end of each unit, students work independently or in cooperative groups to complete critical-thinking and problem-solving activities as well as interdisciplinary projects. These activities integrate skills and connect the theme of each unit to the selections in each unit and to the real world.

Active involvement is the key idea. This text is a hands-on learning experience in which students must read, think, write, and be involved in interdisciplinary activities. All of these skills are set in a thematic environment to make the learning process more meaningful for the student. Learning is the relationship and application of themes and information to daily tasks. Current education research supports the thematic and interdisciplinary approach to teaching and learning.

Organization

Each of the sixteen units is organized into the following components.
- The Theme and its Definition
- The Prereading Activity
- Selections A,B,C and questions after each—vocabulary, comprehension, study skills, writing skills
- Connecting the Theme and Selections activities based on Bloom's Taxonomy
- Applying the Theme to the Real World activities—interdisciplinary projects

Note: The Overview and Practice Unit detail the above organization and should be carefully completed before beginning to use the text.

Also, the A,B,C selections indicate a slight increase in maturity of topic, application of skills, and, to a certain extent, readability levels. These readability levels average 5.0 through 8.0.

Methods for Individual Use

Entire Program. Most students can benefit from proceeding through the entire program, unit by unit and theme by theme, practicing applying the skills in each selection of each unit. When completing the questions and activities for each selection, students should always refer to the selections as needed. This is called "aided recall," and it reinforces the reading comprehension process as well as preparing for tests.

It is important for teachers to recognize that the units may be taken out of sequence or grouped into two or more units for consecutive study. Or a particular unit can be selected for study because it is aligned with curriculum objectives in another subject.

The Themes, the Skills, the Unit Activities

The Themes
Each unit is organized around a theme. The theme is what the whole unit is about. The themes and the selections reflect current and real-world topics that all students encounter today and will encounter in their future world of school and work.

The Skills
Each unit contains four sets of skill activities and questions after each selection.

A. Vocabulary Skills. These three questions focus mainly on developing vocabulary in context and synonym skills.

B. Comprehension Skills. These ten questions practice the same reading skill aligned with the question number according to the following:

1. Locating Facts and Answers
2. Details
3. Sequence
4. Major and Minor Topics

5. Main Idea
6. Comparison/Contrast and Cause/Effect
7. Fact and Opinion
8. Drawing Conclusions and Inferences
9. Reasoning
10. Author's Purpose and Bias

Note: The above skills can be grouped into Literal Comprehension in Questions 1-3, Technical or Interpretive Comprehension in Questions 4-6, and Higher Order Critical Thinking Comprehension in Questions 7-10.

C. Study Skills. These two questions practice outlining and summarizing skills.

D. Writing Skills. These two questions practice sentence and paragraph writing skills.

The Unit Activities

Each unit contains two sets of activities that connect the selections to each other and apply the theme and selections to the real world.

The six activities in *Connecting the Theme and Selections* are modeled after Bloom's Taxonomy for Higher Order Thinking. This model provides six levels of the thought process: Knowledge, Comprehension, Application, Analysis, Synthesis, and Evaluation. Phrased as action verbs (Know, Comprehend, Apply, Analyze, Synthesize, Evaluate), these levels of thinking identify each activity and give students clear-cut direction and goals.

The activities in *Applying the Theme and Selections to the Real World* provide a choice of up to five interdisciplinary projects about the theme in real-world settings.

All of these unit activities can be completed independently or in cooperative groups.

Curriculum, Instruction, Assessment

Current theory and research in education speak to a balance in curriculum—what is taught; instruction—how material is taught; assessment—how learning is measured. *Real World Literacy Skills* provides for a balance of quantitative measurement in the Skills questions after each selection and qualitative measurement in the Unit Activities. Teachers should work toward a balance of the two and recognize that many state assessment programs now provide "open-ended" inquiry questions to measure student mastery of thinking, reading, and writing ability.

TO THE TEACHER

Theory and research also emphasize the "process" of learning as well as the need to integrate the major skills across the curriculum. In today's complex and information-driven society, the emphasis needs to be placed on finding and using information for specific tasks rather than trying to retain volumes of specific facts.

Literacy skills need to be practiced in a variety of activities and assessed in a variety of formats. These formats include answering questions, writing paragraphs, maintaining a journal or portfolio, designing artwork, creating songs and poems, and using interactive computers and technology for research, word processing, graphics, etc.

This book places much emphasis on this variety of approaches to curriculum, instruction, and assessment. The focus is on developing students into life-long and independent learners.

The Reading Selections

The selections present a balance of different kinds of writing: instructional (giving directions), narrative (storytelling), descriptive (describing), and expository (explaining, persuasive—and sometimes opinionated). All of these writing types are presented in a variety of content subjects—language arts, social studies, and science—to provide the student with reading and writing skills in the content subjects. The selections are models of concise and effective writing about current topics. They are intended to capture the student's interest, while improving skills and motivating students to achieve progress in their quality of writing.

Extending the Use of the Selections

Real World Literacy Skills provides many questions and activities for improving literacy skills. In addition to each unit, the following are available for appropriate use in each selection to further enhance the learning experience through integration of skills.

Write your own question and then your own answer for 1-6:

1. Begin your question with the word *Who.*
2. Begin your question with the word *What.*
3. Begin your question with the word *When.*

4. Begin your question with the word *Where.*
5. Begin your question with the word *Why.*
6. Begin your question with the word *How.*
7. What is the main problem discussed in the selection?
8. How is the problem solved?
9. How is this selection about your own life or the world around you?
10. Which sentence in the entire selection is the most important to understanding the theme?

Extended Reading

Literature-based curriculum and reading are the most important ways to reinforce subjects at school and the work we do in our careers. Titles with a major theme in a variety of subjects are available to reinforce the understanding of themes studied in the units of this book. It is recommended that students research a theme further at the library or through computer databases to acquire a bibliography of appropriate literature titles for outside reading during the school year and summer.

The Answer Key

Finally, the Answer Key (a separate pamphlet) serves as a guide. Answers are provided for the four sets of skill questions after each selection. Some answers are either right or wrong because the skill questions are more literal. Other answers are not quite as exact because the questions are more interpretive or inferential. Still other answers give an "example" answer or ask you to "choose an appropriate answer" because several choices are possible, depending on one's viewpoint.

A Final Word

Real World Literacy Skills provides a practical approach to develop literacy skills needed at school and work. These vocabulary, comprehension, study skills, and writing skills are integrated into a thematic and interdisciplinary approach to learning.

TO THE TEACHER

This literacy process is ongoing. It requires instruction, practice, review, and practical application. It is hoped that you will find a significant place for these units and lessons to provide improved literacy development and enhanced learning environments for your students.

CONTENTS

CONTENTS

CONTENTS

CONTENTS

UNIT OVERVIEW

This is the Overview for each unit in the book. Be sure to refer back to these pages, if necessary, as you work through each unit.

Theme ⟶

A **theme** is a topic or subject that is studied or written about.

Definition ⟶

A short definition of the theme is given before you begin to study that theme and unit.

Prereading Activity ⟶

You will then practice a few sample activities about the theme in order to understand it.

Let's practice an entire sample unit from start to finish.

The Theme of
LEARNING

Definition

LEARNING is gaining knowledge through study or experience to understand things and to solve problems.

PREREADING ACTIVITY

1. Think about some of the many things you learn about and where or how you learn about those things.

   a. Subjects such as mathematics and social studies at school from teachers and books
   b. How to play softball or baseball at your local park from coaches
   c. Using a computer through practice at school and at home

2. Now think about some of the specific reasons why learning about these things is so important.

   a. Having information to understand how to solve math problems or understand how our country is governed
   b. Learning a sport to be part of a team and compete against other teams
   c. Using new technology for schoolwork or in a part-time job to earn money for college

Selections A, B, and C

You will then read three different selections about the theme and practice all of the following activities after **each** selection. Remember to always refer back to the selection to find information to complete the questions and activities.

3. Now give three more examples of your own for things you have learned about. Next to each, briefly explain where or how you learned about it and a reason why it is important.

The first two are done for you.

Example 1. How to play a musical instrument in the band at school helps to develop a talent for enjoyment and appreciation of music.

Example 2. Growing a garden in your backyard gives you an understanding and appreciation of how nature works.

Example 3. _____

_____

(Maybe you wrote about learning about the weather or how to drive a car or studying a foreign language or how to be a good neighbor.)

Now carefully read the following selection about the theme of learning.

 **SELECTION A**

The Census Bureau in Washington, D.C., studies many topics. Then this government agency provides important information for the public about those topics. This information might be about the different cost of housing in different parts of the country or where people are moving after they retire. Other information is about career opportunities, the weather, health, recreation, etc.

Some of these census studies might be used by businesspeople to plan for future growth. Other studies might

Practice the Skills ⟶

be used by elected officials in cities and towns to show why theirs is the best city or town to live in. Still other studies might be used by other individuals to learn about which college to attend, what career to enter, or what keeps us healthy and living longer.

A recent report from the Census Bureau is an interesting one. According to the bureau, "The more you learn, the more you earn." A study was done comparing the average American's lifetime earning with his or her education. They found that the higher the education, the higher the earnings.

Think about the following facts. People with a high school diploma earn an average of about 20 thousand dollars a year. People with a college degree average about 35 thousand dollars a year. People with an advanced college degree average over 50 thousand dollars a year.

Over a lifetime, the study said that the average high school graduate will earn a little less than one million dollars, while the college graduate will earn about 1.5 million dollars. The American with an advanced college degree will earn over 3 million dollars in his or her lifetime. Suffice it to say, the students who do not finish high school are at the bottom, earning about 15 thousand dollars a year or a little over a half million dollars in a lifetime—not to mention lost opportunities in the years ahead.

Now, that's "food for thought" to digest as you learn about planning your future.

PRACTICE THE SKILLS

Now carefully read the questions for each set of activities for Selection A. The answers are provided so you can practice an entire set of skill activities before you go on to the questions in Selections B and C. Try to answer each question before you look at the answer. And refer back to the selection at any time to understand the answer.

A. Vocabulary Skills

Three vocabulary questions stress skills such as **context clues** and **synonyms.** You may want to have a dictionary or thesaurus as a reference while completing the vocabulary questions.

B. Comprehension Skills

Ten comprehension questions stress the same skill for each question number according to the following.

Question #1—Locating Facts and Answers

This skill requires you to practice finding information to answer a question.

A. Vocabulary Skills

Circle the letter next to the best answer.

1. The word **bureau** as used in the selection refers to a   (*a*) type of furniture   (*b*) street in a major city   (*c*) government agency (*d*) college graduate.

Notice the context clues of "Washington, D.C." in the first sentence and "this government agency" in the second sentence. These clues tell you that (c) is the correct answer.

2. In the phrase **used by individuals,** the word **individuals** could be replaced best with which of the following words in the selection? (*a*) business   (*b*) students   (*c*) Washington, D.C.   (*d*) cities and towns

Notice that this sentence with the word "individuals" is about people. The context clues of "learn about which college to attend" and "what career to enter" in that sentence point to a synonym about people. These clues tell you that (b) is the correct answer.

3. The last sentence contains the words **food** and **digest** in the phrase **food for thought to digest.** Here, these words are about (*a*) business and profits (*b*) what keeps us healthy and living longer (*c*) high school and college (*d*) information and the mind.

Notice that the sentence is about using this Census study to plan your future. A key context clue is "thought." Thus, the correct answer is (d).

B. Comprehension Skills

1. Remember, the skill is **locating facts and answers.** Information about how much the average American earns each year is located in which paragraph?   (*a*) second   (*b*) third   (*c*) fourth (*d*) fifth

Question #2—Details ⟶

This skill requires you to give specific answers to a question.

Question #3—Sequence ⟶

This skill requires you to practice understanding the order in which events occur.

Question #4—Major and Minor Topics ⟶

This skill requires you to understand how information is grouped according to general and specific information. (It is also a skill needed to master the study skill of outlining.)

Notice that the answer is (c) because the fourth paragraph contains facts about how many dollars are earned by the average American each year.

2. Remember, the skill is **details.**
The average high school graduate will earn about how much in a lifetime?   (*a*) one half million dollars   (*b*) 1 million dollars   (*c*) 1.5 million dollars   (*d*) 3 million dollars

Notice that this skill requires you to locate specific information. The sentence in the selection tells you that the average high school graduate will earn a little less than one million dollars. The answer is (b).

3. Remember, the skill is **sequence.**
What does the Census Bureau do before it provides the public with information about a certain topic?   (*a*) studies that topic   (*b*) moves to a new city or town   (*c*) hires high school graduates   (*d*) locates businesses to complete the study

Notice the first two sentences. The first sentence tells that the Census Bureau studies many topics. The next sentence tells that it then provides information. In the correct sequence of events, the answer is (a). Before it provides information, the Census Bureau studies that topic.

4. Remember, the skill is **major and minor topics.**
The major topic in the selection for the minor topics **businesspeople, elected officials, other individuals** would be people who   (*a*) earn more than 3 million dollars a year   (*b*) live longer   (*c*) use census studies   (*d*) depend on the weather.

Notice that the second paragraph is introduced with a discussion of who uses census studies. Then, specific types of people are mentioned. The major topic would be "people who use census studies." The minor topics would be the specific types of people such as businesspeople and elected officials. Thus, the answer is (c).

Question #5—Main Idea

This skill requires you to understand what the whole selection is about or to choose or create a title for the selection. (It is also a skill needed to master the study skill of summarizing.)

Question #6—Comparison/Contrast or Cause/Effect

This skill requires you to understand how some things are alike or different. Or what causes something to happen and the result (effect) of that happening.

Also notice how the question could be reversed.

Give two minor topics from the selection for the major topic **people who use census studies**. The answer would be **businesspeople and elected officials**.

5. Remember, the skill is **main idea.**
The main idea of the entire selection is about   (*a*) good eating habits   (*b*) time needed for schoolwork   (*c*) the cost of going to college   (*d*) a government study about education and lifetime earnings.

Notice that all of the answers have something to do with the selection. But the main idea is what the whole selection is about. Thus, the answer is (d).

Also notice how a main idea question could be structured around some kind of title format. Titles are short, catchy phrases about a whole selection or story.

Which of the following would be the best title for this selection?
(*a*) Employment Opportunities at the Census Bureau
(*b*) Study Shows the More You Learn, the More You Earn
(*c*) College Graduates Lead Happier Lives
(*d*) Americans Living Longer

Again, all of the above are related to the selection in some way. But (b) is what the whole selection is about.

6. Remember, the skill is **comparison/contrast** or **cause/effect.**
The selection compares   (*a*) living in Washington, D.C. with other cities   (*b*) how long we live with the food we eat   (*c*) average lifetime earnings with amount of education   (*d*) types of high schools and types of colleges.

Notice that the answer is found in the end of the third paragraph. The answer is (c).

Also notice how the question could be asked in a cause/effect format.

11

Question #7—Fact or Opinion ⟶

This skill requires you to recognize and understand information that can be proven true or false (fact) and information that is a belief that cannot be proven true or false (opinion).

Question #8—Drawing Conclusions and Inferences ⟶

This skill requires you to analyze information and use it to answer questions about the theme or the selection.

What is the effect of achieving a college degree for the average American? (*a*) a longer life (*b*) a healthier life (*c*) earning more money (*d*) getting a job in Washington, D.C.

Again, the causes and effects of more education are about money and earnings as described in the selection. The answer is (c).

7. Remember, the skill is **fact or opinion.**
Copy a sample fact from the selection. **The Census Bureau in Washington, D.C., studies many topics.**

Notice that this statement can be proven true. Thus, it is a good example of a fact. Suppose you were asked to rewrite your fact into an opinion.

The Census Bureau in Washington, D.C., studies topics that are important to every American.

Notice how this statement is an opinion that cannot be proven true.

Now let's reverse the question.

Copy a sample opinion from the selection. **A recent report from the Census Bureau is an interesting one.**

Notice how this statement is an opinion because it cannot be proven interesting to everyone. Now rewrite it into a fact.

A recent report from the Census Bureau is available to be read.

Notice how this statement becomes a fact because it can be proven true.

8. Remember, the skill is **drawing conclusions and inferences.**
If a husband and wife were both college graduates, their combined income each year would average about (*a*) 35 thousand dollars (*b*) 50 thousand dollars (*c*) 75 thousand dollars (*d*) 100 thousand dollars

13

UNIT OVERVIEW

Question #9—Reasoning ———————————————→

This skill requires you to then apply information to the theme or solve problems about the theme or predict outcomes.

Question #10—Author's Purpose or Bias ——————————→

This skill requires you to understand why the author wrote the selection (purpose) or what types of attitudes or feelings the author has about the theme or the content of the selection (bias).

Note: Most vocabulary and comprehension questions are constructed with specific multiple-choice answers. Some are constructed for specific short answers. Still others are more open-ended for a variety of answers.

Also note the transition in the comprehension questions. Questions #1–3 are literal comprehension skills. Questions #4–6 are interpretive skills, while #7–10 are critical-thinking skills.

14

Notice that the specific answer to the question is not in the selection. But the selection does say that the average person with a college degree will earn 35 thousand dollars a year. At 35 thousand each, you would conclude or infer that the husband and wife total would be about 70 thousand dollars. Thus, (c) is the correct answer.

9. Remember, the skill is **reasoning.**
You would think that one major problem the study points up is the need to   (*a*) get as many Americans as possible to graduate from high school   (*b*) expand the services of the Census Bureau (*c*) advertise good places to live   (*d*) save money for retirement.

Notice that all of the answers could be correct. But when you examine a problem that comes from the information in the whole selection, the most important need is to at least get people to graduate from high school. This opens up other opportunities. Thus, (a) is the best answer.

10. Remember, the skill is **author's purpose or bias.**
The author wrote this selection to   (*a*) entertain   (*b*) teach (*c*) inform   (*d*) advertise.

Notice that the selection contains much information to give you something to think about. Thus, the author's purpose or reason for writing the selection is to inform you. Answer (c) is correct.

Now let's rephrase the question into a format about author's bias.

How would you describe the author's feelings or beliefs about the study?   (*a*) the amount of learning and school will affect your earnings   (*b*) the more you learn, the happier and healthier you will be   (*c*) high school dropouts can still succeed   (*d*) retirement is a good time to go back to school.

Again, the author wrote the selection to inform the reader about a study about learning and earning. Thus, (a) is the correct answer.

C. Study Skills ⟶

Two study skill questions or activities stress the same skill for each question number according to the following.

Question #1—Outlining ⟶

This skill requires you to use Roman numerals, letters, and sometimes Arabic numbers to organize information from the selection into a framework. (Remember that the skill of major and minor topics is important here.)

C. Study Skills

1. Remember, the skill is **outlining.** (Refer back to the comprehension skill of major and minor topics.)

Let's first look at a sample outline that shows how the framework is structured on the left and how sample information from the selection is entered on the right.

I. **Major topic**
   A. **Minor topic**
      1. **Specific detail**

I. **Census Bureau**
   A. **Studies topics**
      1. **Learning and earning**

Now let's look at one sample outline with information from one part of the selection.

I. **The Census Bureau in Washington, D.C.**
   A. Studies many topics
   B. Provides information to the public about those topics
      1. Cost of housing
      2. Where people are moving
      3. Career opportunities, etc.
   C. People who use this information.
      1. Businesspeople to plan future growth
      2. Elected officials
      3. Other individuals

Now let's look at a second sample outline about the whole selection that is a little more general than the above.

I. **The Census Bureau in Washington, D.C.**
   A. Studies many topics
   B. Provides information to the public
   C. People use the information for different reasons
II. **Facts from one recent study about learning and earning**
   A. High school dropouts earn about 15 thousand a year
   B. High school graduates earn about 20 thousand a year
   C. College graduates earn about 35 thousand a year
      1. Those with advanced degrees earn over 50 thousand

Question #2—Summarizing

This skill requires you to take larger amounts of information and condense them into a few sentences about the selection. (Remember that the skill of main idea is important here.)

D. Writing Skills

Two writing skill questions or activities stress the same skill for each question number according to the following.

Remember that an outline is a simplified framework of organized information for you to use to study for a test or refer to for homework. It should contain only the information that you think is necessary to remember.

2. Remember, the skill is **summarizing.** (Refer back to the comprehension skill of main idea.)
Summarize what the Census Bureau does in one sentence. **The Census Bureau studies topics and then provides information to the public about that topic.**

Notice how the sentence gives as much information as possible about the Bureau without giving a lot of details.

Now let's look at a summarizing question about the whole selection.

Summarize the whole selection in two sentences. **The selection is about the Census Bureau and how it studies topics that might be important to Americans. One recent study showed that the more education you get, the more you will earn each year and in your whole lifetime.**

Also notice that using your outline information from Question 1 can be helpful in answering summarizing questions.

D. Writing Skills

Good sentences and paragraphs stress the 5W pattern of Who, What, When, Where, and Why. A combination of any number of the five in any order makes your writing clearer and more effective.

For example, look at the following model sentence about the selection using the 5W pattern.

You should get as much education as possible in school every year because it will affect your earnings.

19

Question #1—Sentence Writing ⟶

This skill requires you to practice writing complete sentences.

Question #2—Paragraph Writing ⟶

This skill requires you to write and organize several sentences (usually at least four) into one paragraph.

1. Remember, the skill is practicing writing **complete sentences.**
Write one complete sentence telling about students who do not finish high school. Students who do not finish high school will probably not get a good job and will earn less money every year because of less education.

2. Remember, the skill is practicing writing **complete paragraphs** (at least four sentences about the same topic).
Pretend that you are writing an editorial for the newspaper about the importance of learning and getting a good education. Use the selection for information in your editorial paragraph.

> Americans need to get a good education and stay in school as long as possible. The Census Bureau in Washington, D.C. has a study that shows the more you learn, the more you earn. College graduates earn almost twice as much as high school graduates every year. A good education is important because it gives more opportunities for you during your life. So stay in school and aim for college because the study shows that you will be better off in the future.

Now carefully read this second selection about learning. Then answer the questions in each section carefully. Refer to the selection at any time for information to answer any question. After you finish all the questions, check your answers in the back of the book. Then go on to Selection C.

SELECTION B

> Think of all the different kinds of sports. You probably didn't include bird-watching. Think of all the different kinds of books to read. You probably didn't include books about bird-watching.

A. Vocabulary Skills ⟶

Three vocabulary questions stress skills such as **context clues** and **synonyms.** You may want to have a dictionary or thesaurus as a reference while completing the vocabulary questions.

Roger Tory Peterson died a few years ago. He was 87. Roger Peterson may not be the most famous name in history. But he will be remembered by millions as The Birdman of America. He will be remembered as the man who helped people to learn about birds.

Mr. Peterson wrote *Field Guide to Birds* in 1934. To this point, the book has sold some 8 million copies. It has been translated into 12 languages. What the book did was begin a new era of appreciation for wildlife. It contains simple descriptions, pictures, and drawings of 5,000 different birds. This allows people to easily identify the types or species of bird in the outdoors. Peterson also added snippets of information about bird behaviors. He even tries to explain the songs of some birds.

Of course, many people are immune to the appeal of bird-watching. They ask why it is so interesting. Have you ever seen an eagle soar majestically above the mountaintops? Or a tiny hummingbird flutter its wings 10,000 times a minute as it feeds with its needle-like beak?

Maybe you just need to get outdoors with the other 24 million Americans who make at least one trip a year from home to look for and at birds. They are learning about the wonders of the environment. They are cherishing the earth. Just as Roger Tory Peterson wanted.

PRACTICE THE SKILLS

A. Vocabulary Skills

1. The word in the selection that means the same as **species** is (*a*) sports (*b*) languages (*c*) types (*d*) behaviors.

2. The word **soar** as used in the selection could be replaced with the word (*a*) feed (*b*) fly (*c*) dive (*d*) die.

B. Comprehension Skills ⟶

Ten comprehension questions stress the same skill for each question number according to the following.

Question #1—Locating Facts and Answers ⟶

This skill requires you to practice finding information to answer a question.

Question #2—Details ⟶

This skill requires you to give specific answers to a question.

Question #3—Sequence ⟶

This skill requires you to practice understanding the order in which events occur.

Question #4—Major and Minor Topics ⟶

This skill requires you to understand how information is grouped according to general and specific information. (It is also a skill needed to master the study skill of outlining.)

Question #5—Main Idea ⟶

This skill requires you to understand what the whole selection is about or to choose or create a title for the selection. (It is also a skill needed to master the study skill of summarizing.)

Question #6—Comparison/Contrast or Cause/Effect ⟶

This skill requires you to understand how some things are alike or different. Or what causes something to happen and the result (effect) of that happening.

3. In the sentence **They are cherishing the earth,** the word **cherishing** means   (*a*) disliking   (*b*) destroying   (*c*) remembering (*d*) loving.

B. Comprehension Skills

1. You would locate the most information in the selection about *Field Guide to Birds* in which paragraph?   (*a*) first   (*b*) second   (*c*) third (*d*) fourth

2. How many different types of birds are described in Mr. Peterson's book?   (*a*) 87   (*b*) 12   (*c*) 5,000   (*d*) 10,000

3. Which of the following events DID NOT occur since 1934?   (*a*) *Field Guide to Birds* has sold 8 million copies.   (*b*) More Americans are into bird-watching.   (*c*) Roger Peterson died.   (*d*) Roger Peterson wrote a second book.

4. The major topic for the minor topics **descriptions, pictures, drawings** is   (*a*) things in Peterson's book   (*b*) things people write when bird-watching   (*c*) things contained in all books about nature (*d*) wonders of the environment.

5. The main idea of the entire selection is about   (*a*) the importance of nature and birds   (*b*) eagles and hummingbirds   (*c*) a man who influenced bird-watching   (*d*) how to write a book.

6. The major effect of *Field Guide to Birds* is   (*a*) it became a TV documentary   (*b*) more Americans learn about and watch birds (*c*) more foreign tourists visit America to watch birds   (*d*) the earth is safer for animals and birds.

Question #7—Fact or Opinion

This skill requires you to recognize and understand information that can be proven true or false (fact) and information that is a belief that cannot be proven true or false (opinion).

Question #8—Drawing Conclusions and Inferences

This skill requires you to analyze information and use it to answer questions about the theme or the selection.

Question #9—Reasoning

This skill requires you to then apply information to the theme or solve problems about the theme or predict outcomes.

Question #10—Author's Purpose or Bias

This skill requires you to understand why the author wrote the selection (purpose) or what types of attitudes or feelings the author has about the theme or the content of the selection (bias).

Note: Most vocabulary and comprehension questions are constructed with specific multiple-choice answers. Some are constructed for specific short answers. Still others are more open-ended for a variety of answers.

Also note the transition in the comprehension questions. Questions #1–3 are literal comprehension skills. Questions #4–6 are interpretive skills, while #7–10 are critical thinking skills.

C. Study Skills

Two study skill questions or activities stress the same skill for each question number according to the following.

Question #1—Outlining

This skill requires you to use Roman numerals, letters, and sometimes Arabic numbers to organize information from the selection into a framework. (Remember that the skill of major and minor topics is important here.)

7. Copy one fact about Roger Peterson and one fact about *Field Guide to Birds*. Then rewrite one of your facts into an opinion.

Fact #1 _____

Fact #2 _____

Opinion _____

8. Most people use Roger Peterson's book to   (*a*) study for tests in school   (*b*) identify birds they see outdoors   (*c*) learn bird songs   (*d*) learn how to become a better artist.

9. You would think that people who are bird-watchers   (*a*) are not interested in sports   (*b*) enjoy nature and the environment   (*c*) have known Roger Peterson   (*d*) travel a lot.

10. Why did the author write this selection?   (*a*) to recognize the contributions of one man   (*b*) to get more people to buy *Field Guide to Birds*   (*c*) to get interested in bird-watching himself   (*d*) to save endangered species of birds.

C. Study Skills

1. Complete the following outline with information from the selection.

I. Some facts about Roger Tory Peterson

A. _____

B. _____
C. Wrote *Field Guide to Birds* in 1934
II. Some facts about *Field Guide to Birds*
A. 8 million copies sold

B. _____

C. _____

D. _____

E. _____

Question #2—Summarizing

This skill requires you to take larger amounts of information and condense it into a few sentences about the selection. (Remember that the skill of main idea is important here.)

D. Writing Skills

Two writing skill questions or activities stress the same skill for each question number according to the following.

Question #1—Sentence Writing

This skill requires you to practice writing complete sentences.

Question #2—Paragraph Writing

This skill requires you to write and organize several sentences (usually at least four) into one paragraph.

2. Summarize the entire selection by completing the following sentence.

Roger Tory Peterson _____

_____

D. Writing Skills

1. Write one complete sentence about why you think people like to watch birds by completing the following. **People like to watch birds because** _____

_____

2. Write at least four sentences describing how bird watching could become a sport. Include some rules that would have to be followed.

_____

_____

_____

_____

Carefully read this final selection about learning. Refer to the selection as needed to answer the questions. After you finish all the questions, check your answers in the back of the book.

 # SELECTION C

    The most important industry throughout American history is agriculture or farming. Into the 21st century, agriculture will likely expand to include aquaculture or

UNIT OVERVIEW

farming in the ocean. Scientists are learning more about how to "grow" fish in the ocean, just as we grow other food supplies on land.

Why? Because the fishing industry has problems. For many years our ocean boundaries, especially the Georges Bank area of the Atlantic, have been overly fished by both Americans and foreigners. What was once an industry of small boats and rugged people carving out a living became a big business. Huge fishing trawlers with massive nets dragged millions of tons of fish each year. There was no regard for the time it takes nature to replace these ocean creatures.

The American government got involved. It imposed laws and programs on the fishing industry. One was mileage limits. These prohibit foreign vessels from fishing within 200 miles of American shores. Another law reduced the number of fishing days a year. This has reduced the amount of catch and profits. But the once-rich fishing grounds off New England are still not replenishing to meet the demand.

A major government program is the boat buy-back programs. People use the money from the sale of their fishing boat to retrain for new jobs.

Are these actions too late?

Hopefully not. The new industry of aquaculture is before us. New businesses would purchase parcels of ocean from the government. These would become "fish farms." These farms would expand the growing of fish from the current species such as salmon on the West Coast to include cod, haddock, and flounder in the Atlantic Ocean off the East Coast. Technology would be used to improve the farming techniques in the ocean. Huge "pens" would be built to grow and contain the fish from birth to harvest. Even lobster farming is being discussed. These fish farms could even become tourist areas. There, all of us could learn about this new industry.

It is expected that the fishing industry will be a 100 billion dollar business by 2010. That's a lot of jobs for a lot of Americans. Not to mention the guaranteed supply of a quality food.

A. Vocabulary Skills

Three vocabulary questions stress skills such as context clues and synonyms. You may want to have a dictionary or thesaurus as a reference while completing the vocabulary questions.

B. Comprehension Skills

Ten comprehension questions stress the same skill for each question number according to the following.

Question #1—Locating Facts and Answers

This skill requires you to practice finding information to answer a question.

Question #2—Details

This skill requires you to give specific answers to a question.

Question #3—Sequence

This skill requires you to practice understanding the order in which events occur.

Question #4—Major and Minor Topics

This skill requires you to understand how information is grouped according to general and specific information. (It is also a skill needed to master the study skill of outlining.)

PRACTICE THE SKILLS
☑

A. Vocabulary Skills

1. You would guess that the prefix **aqua-** on the word **aquaculture** means   (*a*) future   (*b*) land   (*c*) water   (*d*) money.

2. **Trawlers** are   (*a*) boats   (*b*) trucks   (*c*) planes   (*d*) fishing nets.

3. The best word to replace the word **replenishing** as used in the selection is   (*a*) removing   (*b*) replacing   (*c*) refunding (*d*) restructuring.

B. Comprehension Skills

1. Copy one sentence from the selection that contains the answer to

   the following question. **What area has been overfished?** _____

   _____

2. In addition to growing fish, what other type of seafood is mentioned for possible harvest?   (*a*) oysters   (*b*) crabs   (*c*) shrimp   (*d*) lobsters

3. Which of the following happened after the government got involved in the fishing industry?   (*a*) The price of fish decreased.   (*b*) Fishing days were increased.   (*c*) Boat buy-back programs were started. (*d*) Tourist areas were built.

4. The best minor topics from the selection for the major topic **species of fish in the Atlantic** is   (*a*) jobs, tourist areas, quality food (*b*) cod, haddock, flounder   (*c*) salmon and lobster   (*d*) boats, trawlers, nets.

Question #5—Main Idea

This skill requires you to understand what the whole selection is about or to choose or create a title for the selection. (It is also a skill needed to master the study skill of summarizing.)

Question #6—Comparison/Contrast or Cause/Effect

This skill requires you to understand how some things are alike or different. Or what causes something to happen and the result (effect) of that happening.

Question #7—Fact or Opinion

This skill requires you to recognize and understand information that can be proven true or false (fact) and information that is a belief that cannot be proven true or false (opinion).

Question #8—Drawing Conclusions and Inferences

This skill requires you to analyze information and use it to answer questions about the theme or the selection.

Question #9—Reasoning

This skill requires you to then apply information to the theme or solve problems about the theme or predict outcomes.

Question #10—Author's Purpose or Bias

This skill requires you to understand why the author wrote the selection (purpose) or what types of attitudes or feelings the author has about the theme or the content of the selection (bias).

C. Study Skills

Two study skill questions or activities stress the same skill for each question number according to the following.

Question #1—Outlining

This skill requires you to use Roman numerals, letters, and sometimes Arabic numbers to organize information from the selection into a framework. (Remember that the skill of major and minor topics is important here.)

5. Copy one sentence that you think tells a lot about the entire

selection. _____

_____

6. The selection compares the industry of growing of fish in the ocean with   (*a*) farming   (*b*) tourism   (*c*) boating   (*d*) dining out.

7. In the following sentence, which word makes the sentence more of an opinion than a fact? **Into the 21st century, agriculture will likely expand to include aquaculture or farming in the ocean.** (*a*) century   (*b*) likely   (*c*) include   (*d*) ocean

8. Which of the following must be most available for successful aquaculturing?   (*a*) computers   (*b*) food for fish   (*c*) ocean water (*d*) tourists

9. Aquaculture is intended to create more   (*a*) tourism and smaller boats   (*b*) fishing days and higher boat prices   (*c*) government programs and help for foreign fisherman   (*d*) fish supplies and jobs.

10. The author wrote this selection to   (*a*) entertain   (*b*) inform (*c*) warn   (*d*) give directions.

C. Study Skills

1. Complete the following outline with information from the selection.

I. Problems I learned about in the fishing industry
   A. Over fishing by Americans and foreigners

   B. _____

   C. _____

Question #2—Summarizing ⟶

This skill requires you to take larger amounts of information and condense it into a few sentences about the selection. (Remember that the skill of main idea is important here.)

D. Writing Skills ⟶

Two writing skill questions or activities stress the same skill for each question number according to the following.

Question #1—Sentence Writing ⟶

This skill requires you to practice writing complete sentences.

II. Government laws and programs I learned about in the fishing industry
   A. Mileage limits

   B. _____

   C. _____

III. _____
   A. New businesses would purchase parcels of ocean from the government

   B. _____

   C. _____

   D. _____
   E. New jobs and quality food will be provided

2. Summarize the major reason why you think aquaculture will expand as a new business into the 21st century. **I think that aquaculture**

will expand because _____

_____

D. Writing Skills

1. Write one complete sentence about the fishing industry using the 5W pattern of Who, What, When, Where, and Why in any order.

_____

_____

Now rewrite the sentence, changing the order of the 5W's.

_____

_____

Question #2—Paragraph Writing

This skill requires you to write and organize several sentences (usually at least four) into one paragraph.

Unit Activities

There are two sets of Unit Activities.

A. The first set of activities connects the theme and selections. There are six activities that follow Bloom's Taxonomy of Higher Order Thinking—Knowledge, Comprehension, Application, Analysis, Synthesis, and Evaluation. Be sure that all six activities are completed in sequence.

2. Write at least four sentences describing two good jobs that will probably be important in the aquaculture industry. _____

_____

_____

_____

Now let's practice a sample set of Unit Activities. The first set of activities connects the theme and selections. The second set of activities contains projects that apply the theme and selections to the real world. All of these activities involve critical thinking. Reread the three selections before you begin each set of activities and refer to any of the selections for information as needed to compete the activities. You may complete these activities independently or in cooperative groups.

Unit Activities

(Note that sample answers or explanations for this set of activities are provided at the back of the book after you complete the entire set.)

Connecting the Theme and Selections

1. Know. Tell the subject or topic you learned about in each selection. The first is done for you.

In Selection A, I learned about studies that show the more you learn in school, the more you earn in your lifetime.

In Selection B, I learned _____

In Selection C, I learned _____

B. The second set of activities applies the theme and selections to the real world. Five different interdisciplinary projects from which to choose are presented.

2. **Comprehend.** Summarize which selection has the most effect on the most people and give one reason for your choice. _____

_____

3. **Apply.** Match one or two pictures from a newspaper or magazine to the topic in one of the selections.

4. **Analyze.** Contrast or tell the difference between two jobs in the aquaculture industry of Selection C. Which one will require more education or provide more lifetime income as described in Selection A?

5. **Synthesize.** Compose a song or write a poem about bird-watching or fish farming and its benefits.

6. **Evaluate.** Predict what your career or job will be and what you will need to learn for that career or job. Also include a discussion of your expected yearly or lifetime earnings. Complete your discussion in paragraph form or on audio or video tape.

Applying the Theme and Selections to the Real World

In these activities you will work on interdisciplinary projects. Use a variety of newspapers, magazines, and other reference materials to complete your choice of the following projects or those assigned to you. Also consider using CD-ROM encyclopedias and other on-line databases as well as television programs and videos to get information for your projects.

(Note that there are no answers for these activities. They are projects that require work in a variety of approaches.)

Interdisciplinary Project 1

Choose a favorite topic or subject that you learned about in school. List at least ten things you learned about that topic or subject. Then choose the most important of the ten things and explain why it is the most important to the overall topic or subject.

UNIT OVERVIEW

Interdisciplinary Project 2

Make a collage of five different jobs or careers. Include those with different types and amounts of education and with different levels of income.

Interdisciplinary Project 3

Watch a program on the Discovery Channel, Learning Channel, or comparable programming about a new industry or business that is emerging. Prepare a written report describing the new business, why it is beginning, and how it will affect America in the way of jobs and services.

Interdisciplinary Project 4

Review the jobs section of a major newspaper. Create an outline of three different levels or groups of jobs with three different levels of income and education requirements. Cut out three specific jobs for each level or a total of nine and paste them onto your outline. Summarize the average yearly and lifetime incomes for each group.

Interdisciplinary Project 5

Describe a favorite hobby, pastime, sport, or activity that you have learned more about over years and that you enjoy. What are some of the specific things you needed to learn? Give several specific reasons why you enjoy this activity.

UNIT 1

The Theme of ADDICTION

ADDICTION is being too dependent on a habit or a practice.

PREREADING ACTIVITY

1. Think about people you know who are "hooked" on doing the same thing to a point where they can't change the habit or practice.

   a. Playing video games
   b. Running ten to twenty miles every day, regardless of weather or other conditions
   c. Eating junk food

2. Think about the reasons why people become addicted to such habits or practices.

   a. Not involved enough in other activities
   b. Training for marathons
   c. Lack of awareness of good diet habits or boredom

3. Now give two examples of addiction that you have observed and a reason for the addiction.

A first example is done for you.

Example 1. A student spends all free time practicing with a band instead of completing school assignments and thinks it will lead to being accepted by the band and being popular at school.

Example 2. _____

_____

Example 3. _____

_____

 **SELECTION A**

Steve watches television at least six hours every school day and more on weekends. Minutes after arriving home from school, he switches on the TV. He keeps watching until midnight, when his mother demands that he turn the set off. The gamut of Steve's viewing ranges from soaps to sports to special news programs. With the remote control, Steve surfs the channels, searching for the perfect program. He never spends more than a few minutes watching any program.

Steve's mother is very concerned. She leaves for work early in the morning and is home by six. She remembers Steve's elementary school years as problem-free. But ever since middle school, he has been spending most of his free time watching television. Once he played kickball, stickball, and twenty-one basketball after school and on weekends. Now he sits alone in front of the TV. No one calls, and he hardly moves.

Last year Steve's mother bought him a computer and joined an on-line service. She hoped to pry him away from television. But the novelty quickly wore off, and Steve's TV time increased.

Steve's mother realizes that her son is a sitting statistic: The average young American spends more time in front of the TV set than in school. She needs some kind of action plan.

Last week she met with Steve's high school principal, his guidance counselor, and some of his teachers. They made three recommendations: Steve should use the library after school, participate in intramural sports, and find a part-time job on weekends.

Steve and his mother have drawn up an informal contract. It requires equal time for watching TV and doing other activities. Once a day, Steve and his mother will spend time together with the TV off. Once a week, Steve will participate in an after-school activity. Once every weekend, they will eat out together or go to a movie or a school sports event.

ADDICTION

If a child has a problem, parents first need to recognize that the problem exists. Then they can discuss possible solutions and decide on a plan of action. These three steps are often the best gifts parents can give to a child.

PRACTICE THE SKILLS
☑

A. Vocabulary Skills

Circle the letter next to the best answer.

1. The word **gamut** refers most closely to what other word used in the same sentence? (*a*) programs (*b*) viewing (*c*) ranges (*d*) soaps

2. The word **surfs** as used in the phrase **surfs the channels** refers to all of the following EXCEPT the (*a*) ocean (*b*) television (*c*) programs (*d*) addiction.

3. In the phrase **But the novelty quickly wore off,** the word **novelty** is replaced best with the word (*a*) price (*b*) fascination (*c*) time (*d*) playing.

B. Comprehension Skills

1. Copy the sentence that answers the question, **With whom did Steve's mother meet to discuss the television problem?**

_____

_____

2. What did Steve's mother buy in an attempt to get him to watch less television? (*a*) basketball hoop (*b*) movie passes (*c*) baseball tickets (*d*) computer

3. Which of the following occurred after the elementary grades? (*a*) Steve got involved in baseball. (*b*) Steve became a computer expert. (*c*) Steve watched less television. (*d*) Steve had fewer phone calls.

4. The best major topic for the minor topics **soaps, sports, special documentaries** is (*a*) movies (*b*) television programs (*c*) school events (*d*) statistics.

5. The main idea of the selection is
(*a*) high school student needs physical fitness program.
(*b*) schools should provide more activities for students.
(*c*) mother deals with son's addiction to television.
(*d*) government does study of children's television programming.

6. According to information in the selection, if you spent thirty hours a week in school, the average young American spends about how many hours watching television? (*a*) about twenty (*b*) more than thirty (*c*) more than sixty (*d*) about one hundred

7. Most of the selection consists of (*a*) observation (*b*) research (*c*) information from books (*d*) information from people.

8. What seems to be the most important factor in beginning to solve the problem of Steve's addiction? (*a*) the informal contract (*b*) the meeting with school officials (*c*) increasing the use of the phone (*d*) punishment for watching TV after school

9. Give two reasons why you think that Steve's mother is a concerned parent.

_____

_____

10. The author seems to show concern and support for which of the following groups? (*a*) working parents (*b*) television companies (*c*) government agencies (*d*) concerned neighbors

Explain your answer. _____

_____

ADDICTION

C. Study Skills

1. Complete the following outline with information from the selection.

    I. Advice from the school officials
       A. After-school use of the library

       B. _____

       C. _____

   II. _____
       A. Equal balance of hours between TV and other activities

       B. _____

       C. _____

       D. _____

2. Summarize the major reason Steve's mother is concerned about him watching too much television. _____

_____

_____

_____

_____

D. Writing Skills

1. Copy the sentence from the selection that you think best tells about the theme of addiction. Write one sentence of your own to explain your choice.

_____

_____

_____

_____

2. Write a letter to the principal from Steve's mother of at least four sentences requesting a meeting to discuss the problem. Include a few reasons for the meeting.

_____

_____

_____

_____

_____

_____

 # SELECTION B

No "butts" about it, the campaign to wipe out cigarette smoking in America is underway. Doctors and scientists say that smoking is one of the most addictive habits. The nicotine contained in cigarettes is actually a drug. Smokers' brains crave repeated doses of nicotine, which makes them feel energetic. In the long run, however, nicotine causes loss of energy.

Medical experts used to focus on the harmful effects of cigarettes only on smokers. Now they know that smoking is also harmful to nonsmokers. When others are smoking nearby, nonsmokers breathe in passive, or secondhand, smoke.

Here are some facts about cigarette smoking and its effects.

Facts About Smoking in the United States

1. Smoking causes 30 percent of all cancer deaths.
2. Smoking causes 87 percent of all lung cancer deaths.

3. Every year more than three thousand nonsmokers die from lung cancer.
4. Every day nine million children under the age of five breathe secondhand smoke at home.
5. Of the two million children with asthma, 20 percent have severe asthma attacks caused by secondhand smoke.
6. Nearly all fifty states have laws against smoking in public buildings.
7. Every year billions of dollars are lost when workers are absent because of smoking-related illnesses.
8. Health insurance costs more because the companies must pay for smoking-related illnesses.
9. Many states are suing tobacco companies to recover their medical costs for smoking-related illnesses.
10. A person who smokes two packs of cigarettes a day for forty years spends more than $60,000 on cigarettes.

Effects of Smoking

1. Cancer, especially lung cancer and throat cancer
2. Heart disease
3. Frequent sickness (colds, asthma, pneumonia, ear infections)
4. Difficulty breathing and a bad cough
5. Irritated eyes, bad breath, stained fingers and teeth, wrinkled face
6. Smelly clothes and hair
7. Less ability to smell and taste
8. Loss of energy and stamina
9. Premature babies (babies born before nine months) to mothers who smoke
10. House fires

Do these facts convince you that cigarette smoking is a major health hazard? What should be our course of action?

PRACTICE THE SKILLS

A. Vocabulary Skills

1. What is **nicotine**? _____

_____

2. One thing that is commonly **inhaled** is   (*a*) food   (*b*) air   (*c*) colors
(*d*) money.

3. The best word to replace the word **hazard** as used in the phrase
health hazard is   (*a*) addiction   (*b*) solution   (*c*) expert   (*d*) danger.

B. Comprehension Skills

1. Copy the sentence that tells how many nonsmokers die each year

from lung cancer. _____

_____

2. Secondhand smoke inhaled by a nonsmoker is called what kind of
smoke?   (*a*) asthma   (*b*) passive   (*c*) premature   (*d*) stamina

3. Asthma attacks may begin   (*a*) before a loss of stamina   (*b*) before
birth   (*c*) after inhaling secondhand smoke   (*d*) after forty years of
smoking.

4. List three minor topics from the selection for the major topic **effects
of smoking.** _____

5. Write a main idea of your own. Begin the main idea sentence or

phrase with the word **smoking.** _____

6. The major health effect caused by smoking is   (*a*) premature births
(*b*) pneumonia   (*c*) lung cancer   (*d*) heart disease.

Explain your answer using information from the selection. _____

_____

7. Copy one of the ten facts about smoking and rewrite it as an opinion.

_____

_____

8. Smoking in America is a money issue as well as a health issue. Explain this statement using information from the selection.

_____

_____

9. The most successful campaign to reduce smoking will have to begin in (*a*) hospitals   (*b*) schools   (*c*) insurance companies   (*d*) courtrooms.

Explain your answer. _____

10. The author probably thinks which of the following are most to blame for the problem of smoking in America?   (*a*) medical experts (*b*) mothers   (*c*) tobacco companies   (*d*) convenience stores

Explain your answer. _____

_____

_____

C. Study Skills

1. Complete the following outline.

   I. Five things I learned about smoking from the selection

      A. _____

      B. _____

      C. _____

      D. _____

      E. _____

  II. Two things I still want to learn about smoking

      A. _____

      B. _____

2. Summarize in one sentence **the major cause of smoking in America.**

_____

_____

D. Writing Skills

1. Write a one-sentence slogan to reduce smoking in America. _____

_____

2. Copy the last two sentences of the selection. Add at least four sentences of your own, recommending how to reduce smoking in America.

_____

_____

_____

_____

_____

_____

 **SELECTION C**

Why do some people become addicted to the alcohol in beer, wine, and liquor? And how can alcoholics be helped? Researchers disagree about what causes alcoholism and how to treat it.

Since the 1960s, many researchers have believed that some people are born with a gene for alcoholism. People who carry this gene are more likely to become alcoholics. Alcoholism, the researchers believe, is a medical condition.

It can be treated with prescription drugs, just as diabetes and high blood pressure are treated. By finding and targeting the gene, medical researchers hope to stop alcoholism.

Now, however, many researchers believe that alcoholism is caused by society, not biology. The factors that cause alcoholism include stressful life events, unemployment, and lack of status in social groups. Many people begin drinking to "drown" their troubles.

These social researchers believe that the most effective treatment for alcoholism is therapy for self-control. Alcoholics will have to find other things in their lives to take the place of drinking. They must also have a strong desire to quit.

Americans who expect a simple solution to the complex problem of alcoholism will be disappointed. There are no easy solutions. Alcoholism may well be caused more by society than by biology. And alcoholics who want to stop drinking will have to develop internal strengths and self-control.

PRACTICE THE SKILLS

A. Vocabulary Skills

1. **Genes** determine a person's (a) new habits (b) inherited characteristics (c) society and environment (d) good fortune.

2. The word **status** as used in the phrase **lack of status in social groups** could be replaced with (a) prestige (b) money (c) treatment (d) problems.

3. What other word in the selection means the same as **therapy**? (a) self-esteem (b) solutions (c) diabetes (d) treatment

B. Comprehension Skills

1. Copy the information that answers the following question. **What are two of the four social and environmental factors that now appear to cause alcoholism?**

_____

_____

_____

2. For many years researchers believed the cause of alcoholism was   (*a*) ulcers   (*b*) diabetes   (*c*) a gene   (*d*) society.

3. In the sequence of modern treatment for alcoholism, the first thing a person needs to do is   (*a*) raise self-esteem   (*b*) reduce self-esteem   (*c*) get a job   (*d*) want to quit using alcohol.

4. The best major topic for the minor topic **alcoholism, diabetes, ulcers** is   (*a*) medical conditions   (*b*) social factors   (*c*) complex problems   (*d*) types of addiction.

5. Choose the best title for this selection.
(*a*) Alcoholism declines in America
(*b*) New gene found to control alcohol
(*c*) New research and new treatment for alcoholism
(*d*) Diabetes and ulcers major health problems

6. The most accurate judgment about alcoholism is that it   (*a*) is incurable   (*b*) is the alcoholic's fault   (*c*) requires proper treatment   (*d*) is easy to cure.

7. Copy the opinion from the selection that you think has the most

impact on the problem of alcoholism. Explain your choice. _____

_____

_____

8. Why do you think that having a good education and a good job might help to prevent a person becoming an alcoholic?

_____

_____

9. Give two specific examples of your own of stressful life events that might cause alcoholism to develop.

_____

_____

10. It is likely that the author   (*a*) uses alcohol   (*b*) knows alcoholics   (*c*) thinks alcoholism is a complex problem   (*d*) wants laws passed to reduce alcoholism.

C. Study Skills

1. Complete the following outline with information from the selection.

I. Some previous beliefs about alcoholism

A. _____

B. _____

C. _____

II. Some new beliefs about causes of alcoholism

A. _____

B. _____

III. Some new forms of treatment for alcoholism

A. _____

B. _____

C. _____

2. Now summarize all of the information from the outline above in two or three sentences. _____

_____

_____

_____

_____

_____

D. Writing Skills

1. Write two or three sentences telling why you think the problem of alcoholism needs attention. _____

_____

_____

_____

_____

2. Now write at least four sentences in paragraph form giving recommendations for treating alcoholism. _____

_____

_____

_____

_____

_____

_____

■ Unit Activities ■

Reread each selection carefully and then complete the following activities independently or in cooperative groups.

Connecting the Theme and Selections

1. **Know.** Name the type of addiction from each selection.

   The addiction in Selection A: _____

   The addiction in Selection B: _____

   The addiction in Selection C: _____

2. **Comprehend.** List three things you still want to know about the theme of addiction.

   _____

   _____

   _____

3. **Apply.** Write a one-paragraph diary entry as though you were a smoker and it is your first day trying to break your addiction.

4. **Analyze.** Analyze how or why Steve in Selection A could experience the addictions in Selection B or Selection C.

5. **Synthesize.** List three common problems or challenges you think people would have breaking an addiction such as those described in the selections.

   Problem 1. _____

   Problem 2. _____

   Problem 3. _____

6. **Evaluate.** Choose the selection that you think shows the theme of addiction with the deepest effect on America today. Answer in paragraph form with one good reason for your choice. Begin with this sentence: **I think that Selection _____ shows addiction with the deepest effect on America today**.

Applying the Theme and Selections to the Real World

Use a variety of newspapers, magazines, and other reference materials to complete your choice of the following projects or those assigned to you. Also consider using CD-ROM encyclopedias and other on-line databases as well as television programs and videos to get information for your projects.

Interdisciplinary Project 1

Write a report about the addiction of gambling. Give some of the types of gambling and several reasons why you think people get addicted to gambling. Then explain why it would be difficult to stop gambling and how this addiction could be stopped.

Interdisciplinary Project 2

Interview an ex-smoker with ten questions. Arrange the results of your interview in question and answer form.

Interdisciplinary Project 3

Create a collage of four drawings showing two other types of addictions that are harmful and two types that are not harmful.

Interdisciplinary Project 4

Research the chemical contents of smoke and alcohol. Write a report containing the major components and the kinds of specific dangers they present.

Interdisciplinary Project 5

Invent a product that would treat an addiction. Name the addiction and write a paragraph that explains the function of the product.

UNIT 2

The Theme of
CHANGE

CHANGE is the act or process of giving a different position, course, or direction to something. It is altering or replacing things and routines.

PREREADING ACTIVITY

1. Think about several examples of changes in your daily life.

    a. Changing clothing
    b. Changing classes at school
    c. Changing TV channels

2. Think of reasons for these changes.

    a. Going to the gym
    b. Starting a new term at school
    c. Looking for a better program

3. Now give one example of your own of a change that is easy to see and of a change that is harder to see. Give a reason for each change.

An example is done for you.

Easy-to-see change. Someone buys a new car because the old one needs costly repairs.

Hard-to-see change. A student joins new clubs at school because she wants to make new friends.

Easy-to-see change. _____

_____

Hard-to-see change. _____

_____

SELECTION A

You are probably reading this somewhere on the continent of North America. (The earth has seven continents, or huge land areas.) Thousands of miles south of where you live lies Antarctica. It is the continent surrounding Earth's South Pole. It is a land of ice, snow, mountains, penguins, and seals. During the winter, Antarctica is almost totally dark and very cold. Some people call it "Earth's last frontier."

Three groups of people are intensely concerned about the future of Antarctica.

First are the scientists. They believe that Antarctica should be a world laboratory. They want to study Antarctica and make plans for its best use for future human beings. They also want to slow the rate of pollution on and around this unspoiled land.

The environmentalists are the second group. They believe that Antarctica should become a world park. It should be protected, they say, from any kind of human impact. They want Antarctica to stay exactly as it is.

Third are the tourists, who visit by plane and ship. They say that Antarctica should remain open to anyone who wants to visit. People from all over the world should be allowed to see its natural beauty and its wildlife. The tourists want to open Antarctica to more overflights and maybe even build runways there.

No one owns Antarctica. But in the 1930s, many countries claimed chunks of Antarctica as their own. These countries wanted to mine the deposits of coal, oil, diamonds, and other minerals that lie below the surface. The United States never claimed territory or recognized others' claims. Instead, the United States built bases for scientific research at the South Pole and in neighboring countries, such as New Zealand.

In 1959, twelve countries signed a treaty. (Another twenty-nine nations have since signed this treaty.) This treaty guarantees that Antarctica will not be used for military purposes. It also guarantees freedom for scientific research. In 1991, twenty-four countries agreed not to do any mining on Antarctica for the next fifty years.

What will become of one of the world's last frontiers?

PRACTICE THE SKILLS

A. Vocabulary Skills

1. The word **protected** as used in the phrase **protected from any kind of human impact** means   (a) destroyed   (b) saved   (c) hurried   (d) claimed.

2. Copy the following sentence and replace the word **deposits** with the best word from the choices that follow. **These countries wanted to mine the deposits of coal, oil, diamonds, and other minerals that lie below the surface.**   (a) tourists   (b) losses   (c) amounts   (d) countries

_____

_____

3. The word **chunks** as used in the phrase **claiming chunks of Antarctica** means   (a) icebergs   (b) bases   (c) frontiers   (d) pieces.

B. Comprehension Skills

1. Copy the sentence that answers the question, **Who owns Antarctica?**

_____

_____

2. Tourists come to Antarctica by   (a) plane and car   (b) car and ship   (c) plane and ship   (d) none of these.

3. What did the United States do in Antarctica? (*a*) built bases (*b*) claimed land (*c*) mined diamonds (*d*) sent tourists

4. One of the three minor topics under the major topic **groups interested about the future use of Antarctica** is **scientists.** What are the other two minor topics? _____

5. This whole selection is mainly about (*a*) the United States (*b*) New Zealand (*c*) Antarctica (*d*) the South Pole.

Now write a title for the entire selection using your answer.

_____

6. What causes tourists to visit Antarctica? _____

_____

7. The second and third sentences in the selection are (*a*) both facts (*b*) both opinions (*c*) a fact and an opinion (*d*) an opinion and a fact.

8. Give one reason why some countries claimed chunks of Antarctica for their own. _____

_____

9. You would reason that the problems related to Antarctica are (*a*) easy to solve (*b*) difficult to solve. Explain your answer using information from the selection.

_____

_____

10. The author of this selection wants the reader to (*a*) make a donation to save Antarctica (*b*) write letters to elected officials to stop building bases on Antarctica (*c*) consider visiting Antarctica (*d*) think about the problems in Antarctica.

CHANGE

C. Study Skills

1. Complete the following outline with information from the selection.

    I. Five things I learned about Antarctica
      A. It is one of the seven continents

      B. _____

      C. _____

      D. _____

      E. _____

2. Summarize the entire selection by completing the following sentence with information of your own. **This selection is about** _____

_____

D. Writing Skills

1. Rewrite the following sentence from the selection as a new sentence of your own without changing the meaning of the sentence. **This treaty guarantees that Antarctica will not be used for military purposes.**

_____

_____

2. Use the last sentence of the selection as the first or topic sentence of a new paragraph of your own. Write at least four sentences, including your opinions.

What will become of one of the world's last frontiers?

_____

_____

_____

_____

SELECTION B

The Constitution of the United States is a very important set of laws. It describes the three branches of the federal government and the powers of each branch. The Founding Fathers signed the Constitution in 1787, and it became law in 1788, when nine of the thirteen states ratified (approved) it.

The first ten amendments (changes) to the Constitution are called the Bill of Rights. They grant rights and protections to American citizens. The Bill of Rights became part of the Constitution in 1791, just fifteen years after America's independence from England.

Here is a brief summary of the rights listed in the Bill of Rights:

1. Freedom of religion; freedom of speech and the press; freedom to assemble peaceably and to petition the government
2. Right of citizens to own and bear arms (for the sake of a militia)
3. No soldiers to be housed in citizens' homes in peacetime
4. Freedom from unreasonable searches and arrests
5. No person tried twice for same offense; person need not testify against self; due process of law; just payment for government's taking private property
6. Right to speedy, public jury trial for criminal offense
7. Right to trial by jury for property loss
8. No excessive bail or fines; no cruel and unusual punishments
9. Rights mentioned in Constitution do not deny other rights belonging to the people
10. Powers not specifically given to the federal government belong to the states or to the people

Other amendments have been added to the Constitution since the Bill of Rights. A new amendment becomes a new "right" for every citizen. Each amendment to the Constitution is very important.

For example, Amendment 13 (1865) ended slavery everywhere in the United States at the end of the Civil War. Amendment 14 (1868) states that every person born or naturalized in the United States is a citizen with the full rights of citizenship. Women, however, were not allowed to vote until 1920, when Amendment 19 was passed. One of the amendments that will soon affect you is Amendment 26 (1971), which gives eighteen-year-olds the right to vote.

Two interesting amendments are 18 and 21. Amendment 18 (1919) prohibited the manufacture, sale, or transportation of intoxicating liquors. In 1933, Amendment 21 repealed (canceled) Amendment 18. Can you think of a reason for Amendment 18 and then Amendment 21?

The Constitution and the rights it grants to every American are part of our everyday life. But in many nations, citizens do not enjoy these rights. The Constitution should not be taken for granted.

PRACTICE THE SKILLS

A. Vocabulary Skills

1. The word **Constitution** as used in the selection means a document that spells out (*a*) slavery (*b*) states (*c*) Americans (*d*) rights.

2. The word **Bill** as used in the selection refers to (*a*) a person (*b*) a place (*c*) a thing (*d*) an animal. Explain your answer in one well-written sentence.

_____

_____

3. Which word best replaces **independence** as used in the last sentence of the second paragraph? (*a*) freedom (*b*) war (*c*) escape (*d*) trial

B. Comprehension Skills

1. When were women first allowed to vote in the United States?
(*a*) 1788   (*b*) 1791   (*c*) 1868   (*d*) 1920

2. How many amendments are there in the Bill of Rights?   (*a*) five
(*b*) ten   (*c*) fifteen   (*d*) twenty

3. What is the correct sequence of events from the selection?
(*a*) Amendment 13, Amendment 14, the Bill of Rights
(*b*) the Bill of Rights, independence from England, Amendment 27
(*c*) independence from England, the Bill of Rights, Amendment 13
(*d*) the Bill of Rights, the Constitution, ratification

4. This selection discusses the major topic **Amendments to the United States Constitution.** The first minor topic is the Bill of Rights. Identify the second minor topic discussed in this selection.

Amendments to the United States Constitution
1. The Bill of Rights
2. _____

5. Copy one complete sentence from the selection that you think is a good main idea or a good title. Explain your choice.

_____

_____

6. The best comparison of Amendment 14 and Amendment 19 relates to   (*a*) slavery and civil rights   (*b*) civil rights and voting rights for women   (*c*) voting rights and pay raises   (*d*) none of these.

7. The sentence in the selection **Each amendment to the Constitution is very important** is an opinion. Explain why it is an opinion.

_____

_____

8. You would guess that once an amendment is added to the Constitution, it   (*a*) can never be repealed   (*b*) can be repealed. Explain how you know this.

_____

_____

9. You would reason that which of the following has the most power to change the Constitution according to information in the selection? (*a*) England   (*b*) women   (*c*) the Founding Fathers   (*d*) elected officials. Explain your answer.

_____

_____

_____

10. Do you think the author of this selection is **for** the Constitution or **against** it? Copy one sentence to support your answer.

_____

_____

C. Study Skills

1. Complete the following outline with information from the selection.

   I. Amendments to the Constitution and what each means
     A. Amendment 13 abolished slavery

     B. Amendment 14 _____

     C. Amendments 18 and 21 _____

     D. Amendment 19 _____

     E. Amendment 26 _____

2. Summarize what the Constitution of the United States is in two to three sentences using information from the selection.

_____

_____

D. Writing Skills

1. You are a United States senator and are proposing an amendment to the Constitution. What change would you suggest, or what new right would you propose? Describe your amendment.

_____

_____

_____

2. Write a four- to seven-sentence paragraph about your new amendment. State the amendment clearly in the first sentence. Then give reasons why you think it should be added to the Constitution.

_____

_____

_____

_____

_____

_____

 **SELECTION C**

Suppose you were living in America in the early 1800s. What kind of job would you have? You would likely be working on a farm, as most Americans did then.

CHANGE

Now suppose you were living in the early 1900s. You would probably work in a factory, for a company, or in a store.

But you are living at the end of the 1900s and about to enter a new century. What is in store for you as you plan a job or career?

The New Economy of the twenty-first century will be very different from the economy of the 1900s, just as the 1900s differed from the 1800s. Most people will have several different jobs or careers during their lifetime. Also, most people will be working for small companies or for themselves.

The key words *restructuring* and *downsizing* are important to understanding the New Economy. *Restructuring* means changing the way a business is run. For example, some products might be dropped and new products offered. Or employees might be allowed to work at home with a computer networked to the company and its customers.

Downsizing means having fewer managers and/or employees. The size of companies has been shrinking for some time. In 1982, there was one business in America for every sixteen people. By the mid-1990s, there was one business for every twelve people. Economists predict that companies will continue to shrink. *Downsizing* also refers to hiring fewer full-time employees and more part-time workers and consultants. The goal of both *downsizing* and *restructuring* is to increase profits for the company.

Now that you know something about the New Economy of the twenty-first century, what are your plans for your future job or career?

PRACTICE THE SKILLS

☑

A. Vocabulary Skills

1. The word **store** as used in the second paragraph means   (*a*) a place to buy things   (*b*) to put away   (*c*) a factory   (*d*) none of these.

77

2. According to the selection, **downsizing** means having   (*a*) fewer workers   (*b*) more workers   (*c*) about the same number of workers (*d*) fewer products.

3. The word **consultants** refers to   (*a*) managers   (*b*) customers (*c*) outside advisers   (*d*) the unemployed.

B. Comprehension Skills

1. If you lived in the 1800s, you most likely worked where? ——————

————————————————————————————————————

2. In what year was there one business for every twelve people? ——————

3. What is the correct sequence of jobs since the 1800s?   (*a*) factory, farm, working at home   (*b*) working at home, factory, farm (*c*) factory, working at home, farm   (*d*) farm, factory, working at home

4. The selection contains key words that relate to the New Economy. Under the major topic **Key words in the New Economy** are two words that are minor topics. One of these words is **restructuring.** Give the other words from the selection.

————————————————————————————————————

5. The best main idea phrase that could also be the title of the selection is   (*a*) The New Economy   (*b*) Life in the 1900s   (*c*) Bigger and Better Businesses   (*d*) How to Work for Yourself

6. How would you contrast the 1980s and the 1990s according to the selection?   (*a*) more businesses in the 1980s   (*b*) more businesses in the 1990s   (*c*) more farms than factories in the 1980s   (*d*) more farms than people working at home in the 1990s

7. Copy one sentence that is a fact and contains a number or a date.

————————————————————————————————————

8. You would guess that more people will be working at home in the New Economy because of the progress in   (*a*) farming   (*b*) factories   (*c*) transportation   (*d*) technology.

9. You would reason that the New Economy in the next century will have   (*a*) more small businesses   (*b*) fewer big businesses   (*c*) better communication   (*d*) all of these.

10. The author wants you to focus mostly on   (*a*) studying the past   (*b*) understanding what happened in the 1990s   (*c*) preparing for changes in the future   (*d*) preparing for a return to the good old days. Explain your answer in one well-written sentence.

_____

_____

C. Study Skills

1. Complete the following outline with information from the selection.

    1. Where people have worked in the history of America
       A. Farms

       B. _____

       C. _____

       D. _____

    II. Why people will change jobs and careers in The New Economy

       A. _____

       B. _____

2. Write two or three sentences of your own using information from the selection and information of your own to summarize the selection.

The New Economy will _____

_____

_____

D. Writing Skills

1. Write one sentence that describes the current job or career of a family member.

   _____

   _____

2. Write one four- to seven-sentence paragraph that describes what you think is the ideal job or career. Give two reasons for your choice.

   _____

   _____

   _____

   _____

   _____

   _____

Unit Activities

Reread each selection carefully and then complete the following activities independently or in cooperative groups.

Connecting the Theme and Selections

1. **Know.** Complete the following sentences with the topic discussed in each selection. The first is sentence is completed for you.

   The topic discussed in Selection A is Antarctica.

   The topic discussed in Selection B is _____

   The topic discussed in Selection C is _____

2. **Comprehend.** Identify which selection and its theme of change affects the most people in everyday society today. Explain your answer in one sentence with one specific reason for your choice.

3. **Apply.** Illustrate the theme of change from one selection with a drawing of your own or with a picture from another source.

4. **Analyze.** Compare the theme of change in each selection. Which selection do you think shows change that would most affect you personally? Explain your answer in the following format.

   I think that Selection ____ most affects my life today. The reasons for my answer are:

   A. _____

   B. _____

   C. _____

5. **Synthesize.** Create a one-minute audio- or videotape discussion of change as represented in one of the selections.

6. **Evaluate.** Complete the following sentence with your choice of selection. Then add two or three sentences to support your topic sentence.

   The theme of change as shown in Selection ____ will make the world better. _____

   _____

   _____

Applying the Theme and Selections to the Real World

Use a variety of newspapers, magazines, and other reference materials to complete your choice of the following projects or those assigned to you. Also consider using CD-ROM encyclopedias and other on-line databases as well as television programs and videos to get information for your projects.

Interdisciplinary Project 1

Create a collage of the theme of change with five pictures from newspapers and magazines or with drawings of your own. Each picture or drawing should show a different example of change. Explain the theme of change with one well-written sentence under each picture.

Interdisciplinary Project 2

Choose one of the selections in this unit and write a song about it with references to change as shown in the selection.

Interdisciplinary Project 3

Locate five jobs available in a newspaper. Choose the one you like most. Give three reasons for your choice and three changes that you would have to make in your life today in order to apply for the job in the future.

Interdisciplinary Project 4

List three new amendments to the Constitution you think are necessary now or will be needed in the future. Describe Amendments 28, 29, and 30 and explain when and why they should be adopted.

Interdisciplinary Project 5

Choose one favorite movie, one favorite television program, and one favorite book. Write one four- to seven-sentence paragraph about the major changes that occurred in each.

UNIT 3

The Theme of
COMPETITION

COMPETITION is a rivalry or contest of skill for profit, a prize, or position.

PREREADING ACTIVITY

1. Think about people you have seen competing for some kind of profit, prize, or position.

    a. Football players on two opposing teams
    b. Students taking tests for college admission
    c. Business advertising its product as the best

2. Think about the results of competition for each example.

    a. The action during the game and the final score
    b. The scores on the tests and the acceptance to a college of choice
    c. A business increases profits, which attracts more investors

3. Now give two examples of your own of competition.

A first example is done for you.

Example 1. Two soft drink companies compete for customers with creative television advertisements during the World Series or Super Bowl.

Example 2. _____

_____

Example 3. _____

_____

SELECTION A

This is the day Laura has been waiting for. Today she will submit her poems and writing samples to the review board. This contingent of students, teachers, parents, and administrators will interview all of the students who apply. Then they will choose the next editor-in-chief of *The Inkwell*, Rosemont High's prize-winning newspaper.

Laura is only a ninth grader, two years younger than most of the other applicants. No freshman has ever been editor-in-chief of *The Inkwell*. But most of the writers and editors will be graduating in June, so the review board invited all interested students to apply.

All of the applicants want to maintain the paper's high quality. They know that being *The Inkwell*'s editor-in-chief paves the way to college acceptances and scholarship opportunities. This has been a long tradition at Rosemont High.

Last year Laura was editor-in-chief of her middle school's monthly newspaper. She knows all about desktop publishing and working with printers, and her portfolio contains sophisticated writing samples. But Laura is sure that many of the tenth and eleventh graders are excellent writers and know as much about publishing as she does.

Laura waits nervously for her 10 o'clock interview. After the interviews, the review board will meet all day to read the writing samples and discuss the applicants. Then they will make their decision. In the early evening, the new editor-in-chief will be called. All but one of the applicants will be disappointed.

At 6:45 that night, the phone rings in Laura's home. She had rehearsed for either victory or defeat. Whatever happened, she would thank the review board for the time they had given her. But now there is no time to think.

Laura grabs the phone and utters a weak "Hello."

"Laura?" a voice questions. "Congratulations!"

PRACTICE THE SKILLS

A. Vocabulary Skills

1. The word **contingent** means   (*a*) contest   (*b*) publications   (*c*) group (*d*) class.

2. The word **utters** means   (*a*) thinks   (*b*) says   (*c*) laughs (*d*) hears.

3. The word **sophisticated** as used in the phrase **sophisticated writing samples** means   (*a*) reviewed   (*b*) awaited   (*c*) advanced (*d*) submitted.

B. Comprehension Skills

1. Copy the phrase that answers the question, **What is *The Inkwell?***

   _____

2. What position was Laura competing for?   (*a*) cheerleader (*b*) freshman class president   (*c*) school newspaper editor (*d*) teacher assistant

3. Which of the following events did NOT occur after the morning interviews?   (*a*) a review of her portfolio   (*b*) lunch with the review board   (*c*) a phone call   (*d*) being selected

4. Give two minor topics from the selection under the major topic

   tradition at Rosemont High. _____

5. Write a title for this selection. _____

6. The major difference between Laura and most of her competitors is (*a*) age   (*b*) ability   (*c*) maturity   (*d*) popularity.

7. Rewrite the following fact into an opinion. **Last year Laura was editor-in-chief of her middle school's monthly newspaper.**

_____

_____

8. Who was on the review board?_____

_____

9. Which one of the following is NOT a reason why so many students competed for the position?   (*a*) maintain the quality of the paper   (*b*) college opportunities   (*c*) college scholarships   (*d*) good-paying part-time job

10. The author is biased toward the underdog. Explain this statement

with specific references from the selection. _____

_____

_____

_____

C. Study Skills

1. Outline the following with specific information from the selection.

    I. Events during the day
      A. Laura submits her portfolio

      B. _____

      C. _____

      D. _____

2. Summarize the contents of Laura's portfolio by completing the

following. **Laura's portfolio** _____

_____

D. Writing Skills

1. Write what you think would be Laura's closing sentence during the interview with the review board by completing the following. **I think that you should choose me because** _____

_____

2. Write at least four sentences that might be part of Laura's acceptance speech. Her audience is *The Inkwell*'s staff of writers and editors. _____

_____

_____

_____

 SELECTION B

Turn back the calendar to February, 1980. Pull out the video of the incredible "miracle on ice" during the Winter Olympics at Lake Placid, New York. Then sit back and enjoy one of the most unbelievable events in Olympic history.

In 1980, a group of amateur hockey players, mostly college students, made up the United States team. They had never played as a team before they began to practice for the Olympics. At that time, Olympic rules allowed only amateur athletes to compete. Professional athletes (those who are paid for their services) could not enter Olympic events.

This was an era when most countries kept their amateur hockey teams playing together for years. This was especially true in Communist countries. The Russian team, for example, had played together practically all their lives. People called them the Big Red Machine, and they were sure medal winners every four years. The gold-medal ceremony seemed to be planned even before the games began.

But not in 1980. Lake Placid rocked and rolled as the

young American team moved through the preliminary rounds and into the medal rounds. Coach Herb Brooks, captain Mike Eruzione, and goalie Jim Craig led the American team.

On a Friday night in late February, the Americans played an incredible semifinal game against the Russians. The winner would play Finland in the gold-medal game on Sunday. In the middle of the third period, the score was tied at 2–2. Eruzione took a pass through center ice, moved over the blue line, and shot a thirty-footer that sent Americans into wild celebration. The score stayed at 3–2 for the next ten minutes, as Craig fiercely guarded the American goal. With seconds counting down, announcer Al Michaels bellowed through his microphone, "Do you believe in miracles?"

On Sunday morning, the American team matter-of-factly beat Finland to win the 1980 Olympic Gold Medal in ice hockey. At the medal ceremony that afternoon, the American national anthem played, American flags waved, and tears streamed down the cheeks of millions. A group of American college students had won the hearts of a nation—and much of the world.

PRACTICE THE SKILLS

A. Vocabulary Skills

1. The opposite of **amateur** as used in the selection is   (a) athlete   (b) professional   (c) announcer   (d) student.

2. The word **era** as used in the selection refers to   (a) time   (b) place   (c) people   (d) the Olympics.

3. The word **bellowed** as used in the selection refers to which sense?   (a) sight   (b) sound   (c) touch   (d) taste

   What context clue word in the sentence helped you get the answer?

COMPETITION

B. Comprehension Skills

1. Where were the 1980 Winter Olympic Games played? _____

2. Who was the coach and who was the captain of the American team?

   _____

   _____

3. What event happened first after the American team beat the Russian team?   (a) the gold-medal ceremony   (b) they played Finland   (c) Eruzione scored a second winning goal   (d) amateur hockey was ended at the Olympics

4. The major topic for the minor topics **anthem played, flags waved, tears streamed** is events   (a) at the opening Olympic ceremony   (b) at the gold-medal ceremony   (c) announced by Al Michaels   (d) in Russia and Finland.

5. Which phrase from the selection is the best main idea for the selection?
   (a) 1980 Winter Olympics
   (b) miracle on ice
   (c) amateur hockey players
   (d) gold-medal ceremony

6. One of the major reasons for the American victory over Russia after Eruzione's goal was   (a) Al Michaels   (b) a miracle   (c) Jim Craig   (d) the American spectators.

   Explain your answer. _____

   _____

7. The first two sentences in the fifth paragraph are   (a) both facts   (b) both opinions   (c) one fact and one opinion   (d) one opinion and one fact.

8. Which of the following statements best describes the major difference between the American team and the Russian team?

(*a*) The American team had lower salaries than the Russian team.
(*b*) The American team was amateur; the Russian was professional.
(*c*) The American team was less experienced than the Russian team.
(*d*) The American team won more medals than the Russian team.

9. What do you think was Herb Brooks's biggest contribution to the victory over the Russian team and winning the gold medal?

_____

10. Why do you think the author wrote this selection?   (*a*) to increase interest in hockey   (*b*) to increase interest in the Winter Olympics   (*c*) to relate an exciting example of competition   (*d*) to show the greatness of America

C. Study Skills

1. Complete the following outline with information from the selection.

   I. Friday night's events at the 1980 Olympics
     A. America plays Russia in the semifinal game

     B. _____

     C. _____

     D. _____
     E. Al Michael's asks, "Do you believe in miracles?"
  II.
     A. America beats Finland to win the gold medal

     B. _____

2. Summarize in one sentence the American victory over Russia by using four of the 5W's: who, what happened, where, and when.

_____

_____

D. Writing Skills

1. Write the sentence that you think Al Michael's spoke after he asked, "Do you believe in miracles?" _____

_____

2. Pretend that you were a television commentator during the gold-medal ceremony that Sunday afternoon. Write at least four sentences about the 1980 American hockey team. _____

_____

_____

_____

 SELECTION C

Have you ever played the board game Monopoly? Players buy, sell, or trade Boardwalk, Park Place, and other properties and businesses. Their goal is to create a monopoly (complete control of a business or property) in order to wipe out competition.

Let's take a look at the world of American business. What are some of the multimillion- and billion-dollar industries in which businesses compete for your dollars? The list is long. It includes the computer industry, the airline industry, the automobile industry, the home supplies industry, and many others. In these industries, huge companies compete for customers and for higher profits every day. How did these companies become so dominant?

Let's look, for example, at the home supplies industry. Once there were local mom-and-pop hardware stores in most towns and cities. These small stores died a slow death when larger regional stores took away their customers. The larger regional stores bought a wider variety of supplies, bought them in larger quantities, and sold them at lower prices than the mom-and-pop stores did. Owners of mom-and-pop hardware stores couldn't lower their prices to compete because they had to keep up with their overhead. (Overhead includes fixed expenses such as heat, electricity, rent, insurance, and employee wages and benefits.)

So the regional stores gobbled up the local stores, but the superstores were lurking. Superstores first appeared in the 1980s. Venture capitalists (people who have a great deal of money to invest) would pool large sums of partnership funds to open a superstore or two.

Superstores are huge warehouse buildings. Their objectives are simple:

- Buy huge amounts of products to sell.
- Attract a variety of customers by selling a much wider variety of products.
- Mark up prices just enough above cost to sell products as quickly as possible.
- Guarantee lower prices than any competitor.
- Give discounts to business customers.
- Keep overhead low by paying lower wages and giving few employee benefits.
- Advertise special offers every day.
- Stay open for long hours and on weekends.

Above all else, superstores aim to increase their profits so that they can plan an IPO. IPO stands for "initial public offering." This means that the corporation has the approval of government agencies to sell shares in the company.

Once an IPO is approved, the corporation can go public. That is, it can sell stock (shares of its company) to the public on a government-regulated stock exchange, such as the New York Stock Exchange. With the huge sums of money the corporation gets from its sale of stock, it can open more and more superstores. When superstores expand, they gobble up the much smaller regional stores.

A superstore corporation's next move is a buyout or merger. One superbig corporation buys out or merges with a serious competitor. The merger reduces competition and also allows the superstore to expand into world markets. If things go right, the corporation continues to expand, and its profits increase.

PRACTICE AND SKILLS

A. Vocabulary Skills

1. Rewrite the sentence **How did these companies become so dominant?** by replacing the word **dominant** with a new word of your own. _____

_____

2. What does the word **overhead** mean as used in the selection? (*a*) objectives   (*b*) expenses   (*c*) IPOs   (*d*) products

3. The word **pool** as used in the selection means   (*a*) a place   (*b*) a thing   (*c*) an action   (*d*) a sport.

Now use the word **pool** in a sentence of your own with the same meaning.

_____

_____

B. Comprehension Skills

1. In the selection, which of the following topics receives the most space?   (*a*) mom-and-pop stores   (*b*) regional stores   (*c*) superstores (*d*) New York Stock Exchange

95

2. When did the trend of venture capitalists begin? _____

3. What happens after government approval to go public?   (*a*) Stock can be sold.   (*b*) Local stores begin to increase.   (*c*) Overhead is reduced.   (*d*) Industries lose money.

4. Give at least two minor topics from the selection for the major topic **objectives of superstores.** _____

_____

5. Write your own one-sentence main idea for the selection. Include the words **business** and **profits** in your sentence. _____

_____

6. The best result of guaranteeing the lowest prices is   (*a*) advertising increases   (*b*) store hours are shorter   (*c*) employee benefits increase (*d*) products are sold more quickly.

7. Rewrite the last sentence of the selection, changing it from a fact into an opinion. _____

_____

8. You would conclude that superstore owners   (*a*) pay little overhead (*b*) have low advertising costs   (*c*) pay employees low wages and few benefits   (*d*) help local stores to survive.

9. You would reason that a type of downtown business that will survive into the future might be one that sells   (*a*) televisions   (*b*) sporting goods   (*c*) fast food   (*d*) garden supplies.

Explain your answer. _____

_____

10. The author seems to place a lot of emphasis on business (*a*) planning   (*b*) discounts   (*c*) hiring practices   (*d*) warehouses.

C. Study Skills

1. Use information from the selection to complete the following outline.

    I. Five important things about American businesses
       A. They compete for higher profits every day

       B. _____

       C. _____

       D. _____

       E. _____

2. Summarize the purpose of the New York Stock Exchange by completing the following sentence and adding one or two more sentences of your own.

The New York Stock Exchange is _____

_____

_____

D. Writing Skills

1. Write one sentence of your own that could be another objective in order to have a successful business. _____

_____

2. Write at least four sentences describing a superstore that you have visited. Explain how that store is like the superstores described in

this selection. What are some of the differences? _____

_____

_____

_____

_____

Unit Activities

Reread each selection carefully and then complete the following activities independently or in cooperative groups.

Connecting the Theme and Selections

1. **Know.** Name the major topic associated with the theme of competition from each selection. The first topic is done for you.

   In Selection A, the major topic was a girl competing to become editor of the school newspaper.

   In Selection B, _____

   In Selection C, _____

2. **Comprehend.** Discuss which selection has the most impact on your life today. Give at least three reasons for your choice. Use the following format.

   I think that Selection ___ has the most impact on my life today.

   Reason 1 is _____

   Reason 2 is _____

   Reason 3 is _____

3. **Apply.** Illustrate with a drawing of your own or a picture from another source one problem that may arise in one of the selections. Then write a one-paragraph solution for that problem under the picture. An example is done for you.

   Example. In Selection A, Laura may want to have a monthly edition of the paper, instead of quarterly. She has to meet with the principal to discuss the issue.

4. **Analyze.** Examine, in chart form, three things you still want to know after reading each selection. Use the following format of questions. A first example for each selection is done for you.

Three things I still want to know about Selection A.
1. How many hours does a newspaper editor work on one issue?

2. _____

3. _____

Three things I still want to know about Selection B.
1. Who were the team members of the 1980 Olympic hockey team?

2. _____

3. _____

Three things I still want to know about Selection C.
1. What happens when a superstore fails or goes bankrupt?

2. _____

3. _____

5. **Synthesize.** Create a poem of at least eight lines with some rhyme about one of the selections and the theme of competition.

6. **Evaluate.** Predict two positive outcomes and two negative outcomes for American business according to the information in Selection C. A sample of each is done for you.

Positive outcome 1 is more stocks to choose from on the New York Stock Exchange.

Positive outcome 2 _____

Positive outcome 3 _____

Negative outcome 1 is fewer family businesses in local cities and towns.

Negative outcome 2 _____

Negative outcome 3 _____

Applying the Theme and Selections to the Real World

Use a variety of newspapers, magazines, and other reference materials to complete your choice of the following projects or those assigned to you. Also consider using CD-ROM encyclopedias and other on-line databases as well as television programs and videos to get information for your projects.

Interdisciplinary Project 1

Research three memorable sports events since 1960. Write a report that explains the event, the outcome, and some of the reasons why the level of competition was so high. Also include pictures or illustrations of each example.

Interdisciplinary Project 2

Play one complete game of Monopoly. Before you begin, write five strategies that you want to follow to win the game. After the game, summarize how well your strategies worked or why they did not work. Then summarize why you won or lost the game.

Interdisciplinary Project 3

Interview the owner or manager of two different stores or businesses with the following five questions. Chart your answers.
1. What are your major products or services?
2. How long have you been in business?
3. What kinds of benefits do you offer to keep employees?
4. Do your employees enjoy or not enjoy working for you? Why?
5. What are two plans or strategies you have to stay in business and increase profits?

Interdisciplinary Project 4

Imagine that you are a candidate for a school office or are applying for a part-time job in your town. Create a mock interview. Make up several good questions and videotape your answers.

Interdisciplinary Project 5

Choose five different examples of competition from newspapers and/or magazines. Create a collage of the pictures and a summary of how competition relates to each picture.

UNIT 4

The Theme of
CONFLICT

Definition

CONFLICT is a struggle or dispute between two opposing forces that is usually settled over time or with some kind of intervention. There are four types of conflict—self against self, self against another person, self against society, self against nature.

PREREADING ACTIVITY

1. Think about conflicts that you have seen or gone through.

   a. An argument between two motorists over the right-of-way at a traffic light
   b. A group of climbers attempting to reach the summit of Mt. Everest
   c. Being new in a school or job and trying to be accepted into a new social group

2. Think about how the conflict is settled.

   a. Other drivers urge them to move on by honking their horns.
   b. They reach the summit or have to return to base camps because of weather conditions.
   c. You are invited to a weekend cookout given by a classmate or coworker.

3. Now give two examples of your own of conflict and tell how the conflict is settled.

A first example is done for you.

Example 1. A courtroom conflict between the two lawyers is settled by the decision of the jury.

Example 2. _____

Example 3. _____

_____

 ## SELECTION A

My folks said they'd be home by midnight. Oh, how I hate being home alone. Maybe I should just find a good book to read. Or maybe I'll bury myself on the couch under two huge pillows. I'll turn on every light in the house and keep the TV blasting. That way the whole house will look busy and full of people.

Imagine being so afraid that you think someone might be lurking in the shadows in another room, someone waiting and waiting for just the right moment.

Enough of this! I'm just getting myself all upset for no reason.

Wait! What was that? This old house has many creaks and groans, but that was a new one to me. Forget it. The more I think about being afraid, the more fear I produce. I should grow up! A thirteen-year-old shouldn't be so scared. Maybe it's all the scary movies I've seen. Come to think of it, why do I actually pay money to get so scared?

Did I lock all the doors? Maybe I should check them again. Ten chimes of the clock—that means two long hours to go. Don't even think about the fact that they usually arrive an hour later than promised. Maybe I should lock myself in the bathroom. Settle down, will you! That was only the refrigerator motor starting up again.

Why am I doing this to myself? Millions of people are home alone right now. They're all ages, all finding a way to enjoy a Saturday evening. But look at me—I'm shaking. I guess I've read too many newspaper headlines and seen too many movies. Forget about the lady two streets around the corner. Maybe I should just get something to eat in the kitchen.

The kitchen—where is that draft coming from? Is the garage door open? What's that blue light across the street? Is the kitchen window open?

PRACTICE THE SKILLS

A. Vocabulary Skills

1. In the phrase **lurking in the shadows,** the word **shadows** is the context clue for the meaning of **lurking,** which is (*a*) showing (*b*) breathing (*c*) darkening (*d*) hiding.

2. A word that could replace **produce** as used in the selection is (*a*) hide (*b*) sell (*c*) develop (*d*) eliminate.

3. Rewrite the phrase **ten chimes of the clock** and replace the word **chimes** with a new word of your own. _____

B. Comprehension Skills

1. Copy a sentence that answers the question, **How do you know that the speaker is probably alone in the house?** _____

_____

2. How old is the speaker? (*a*) thirteen (*b*) fifteen (*c*) seventeen (*d*) twenty-one

3. What happened after the refrigerator clicked on? (*a*) The clock chimed. (*b*) The speaker turned the TV on. (*c*) The speaker thought about neighborhood lady. (*d*) The parents came home.

4. A good major topic for the minor topics **read a book, turn on the TV, lock the doors, stay in the bathroom, eat** is (*a*) things to do on Saturday night (*b*) things to read about in the paper (*c*) things the speaker thinks of doing to lessen fear (*d*) things that cause crime in the home.

107

5. A good title for this selection is   (*a*) Home Alone   (*b*) Crime for a Dime   (*c*) Frightful Sight   (*d*) Nightmare on Main Street.

6. What caused the speaker to go into the kitchen?   (*a*) a noise   (*b*) the phone rang   (*c*) a neighbor was at the door   (*d*) hunger

7. Write a fact sentence of your own to end the selection. _____

_____

8. You would think that most of the conflict and fear that the speaker has is caused by   (*a*) television reports   (*b*) newspaper headlines   (*c*) imagination   (*d*) illness.

9. A good way to solve the speaker's problem of conflict and fear is   (*a*) take a walk   (*b*) call a neighbor and ask to visit for a while   (*c*) close every window and lock every door   (*d*) call the police.

Give another way of your own. _____

_____

10. The author probably wrote this selection to show the power of   (*a*) peers   (*b*) parents   (*c*) an education   (*d*) the mind.

C. Study Skills

1. Complete the following outline with information from the selection.

   I. The five most important events in the selection in sequence
      A. Ten chimes of the clock

      B. _____

      C. _____

      D. _____

      E. _____

2. Summarize the conflict of the entire selection in one sentence.

_____

_____

D. Writing Skills

1. Complete the following with one or two sentences that describe a personal situation or experience that compares with the selection.

One time, I _____

_____

_____

2. Is the speaker alone, or is there someone in the house? Write at least four sentences with reasons for your answer. _____

_____

_____

_____

 SELECTION B

High schools across America are training groups of students to provide special services. These services are for their peers. The services focus on problem solving, counseling, and leadership. Students who volunteer for the program are trained to understand the causes of conflict. They also learn how to help students when conflicts arise.

The trained students are called peer mediators or peer counselors. They are resources and models of mature behavior. They are called on to help stop conflicts between students or groups of students. They also organize informal meetings to help students better understand each other. When students learn how to work with other students, schools become better places for learning and maturing.

Here's an actual case study of conflict mediation.

Two high school freshmen, Mark and Tim, are playing basketball in a local park. Tim goes for a layup and falls hard on Mark. They both fall to the ground. Mark's knee is hurt in the fall, and he thinks that Tim's action was deliberate. They have words, and a pushing match breaks out.

A few weeks later, Tim taunts Rob, a friend of Mark's. The two threaten each other, then fight.

Several nights later, Rob and his friends go looking for Tim in the park. They find Tim with a group of friends.

A neighbor, seeing the angry young men, calls the police. After dispersing the students, the police contact the high school principal. She calls the teacher in charge of the mediation program. Mark, Tim, and Rob are asked to appear at a mediation session.

At the session, no teachers are present. Two freshmen mediators use their skills and their training. Each of the three students tells his story. The others listen without interrupting. The mediators help the young men understand the negative outcomes of continuing their feud. They point out that spring sports tournaments are about to begin and that all three are on the same baseball team. After an hour and a half of finger pointing and venting emotions, the three shake hands. They agree to meet with the mediators once a week for a month.

Think of a conflict in your school or neighborhood. How could it be settled without becoming a major problem?

PRACTICE THE SKILLS

A. Vocabulary Skills

1. **Peers** as used in the selection are   (*a*) parents   (*b*) teachers   (*c*) administrators   (*d*) students.

2. In the phrase **Tim taunts Rob,** the word **taunts** means
(*a*) compliments (*b*) challenges (*c*) strikes (*d*) invites.

3. The word **mediation** as used in the selection means (*a*) thinking
(*b*) intervention (*c*) organization (*d*) continuation.

Use the word in a sentence of your own. _____

_____

B. Comprehension Skills

1. What are mediation groups trained to do? (*a*) support teachers in
preparing lessons (*b*) patrol corridors for the principal (*c*) help
students with problems (*d*) organize basketball leagues

2. Which outside community group in the selection works with the
school in mediation services? (*a*) lawyers (*b*) police (*c*) bankers
(*d*) veterans

3. Which of the following events happened before Tim and Rob had the
fight? (*a*) Rob and friends go looking for Tim. (*b*) Two mediators
meet with Tim. (*c*) Mark and Tim have a pushing match. (*d*) The
principal gives each a warning.

4. What are the three minor topics in the selection for the major topic

special high school services? _____

5. Write a one-sentence main idea for the entire selection. Begin with

High schools _____

6. The major difference between the two mediation students and the
three boys is (*a*) age (*b*) class rank (*c*) maturity (*d*) athletic
ability.

7. Mark thinks that Tim's action was deliberate. In this sentence,
the word that makes the sentence an opinion is (*a*) thinks
(*b*) action (*c*) was (*d*) deliberate.

Explain your answer. _____

111

8. The type of conflict that seems to create the need for mediation services is self against   (*a*) self   (*b*) another person   (*c*) society   (*d*) nature.

9. In the case study, the person who could have solved the problem early is   (*a*) Mark   (*b*) Tim   (*c*) Rob.

Explain one way that person could have solved the problem. _____

_____

10. Does the author think these services are necessary in high schools? Copy one sentence to support your answer. Then write one sentence

of your own to support your answer. _____

_____

_____

_____

C. Study Skills

1. Complete the following outline with information from the selection.

   I. Types of services available in some high schools
   A. Mediation

   B. _____

   C. _____

   D. _____

   II. What students are trained to do
   A. Understand the causes of conflict

   B. _____

   III. Functions of the student groups
   A. Resources and models of mature behavior

   B. _____

   C. _____

2. Summarize the selection by completing the following sentence. **High school students can contribute to their school by** _____

_____

_____

D. Writing Skills

1. Write two or three sentences that describe the problem-solving and conflict resolution program described in this selection. Begin with

Our school offers services _____

_____

_____

2. Write your own case study of a problem between two or more students in your school or neighborhood. Describe the problem and give a few recommendations for solving the problem. _____

_____

_____

_____

_____

_____

 SELECTION C

January 2, 1971

Dear Mom and Dad,

Writing these letters keeps me from worrying. Well, my second Christmas and New Year's Day have passed and I'm still alive. Just ordinary days, though. There are

113

no holidays in this unhappy country of Vietnam. This war has to end. Every day seems like another twenty-four hours of conflict with the unknown. We're fighting people we don't know, in a culture and country we don't know. The weather has been over 100 degrees in jungles filled with enough species to start your own zoo. Two guys were killed New Year's Eve when an automatic explosive device placed by our guys detonated accidentally. Last week was the worst firefight for our platoon in the past eight months. I was scared to death. We lost five men in a fight where nobody ever saw the enemy on either side.

I'm sitting on the jungle floor as I write this. Everything I own or plan to eat is on my back. The only thing you hold most of the day is your gun. Every four days, new supplies arrive by helicopter. I'll never complain about cold leftovers again. That's a promise! The day is spent tramping around the jungle till noon, set up camp, talk, and go to sleep—or try to. Next Tuesday is day twenty. Every twenty days, a helicopter picks us up and off we go to a central camp with showers, hot food, and five days of rest. Then back to the jungle. Rumor has us pulling guard duty at Bien Hoa, starting in March. May 1 is the target date for all jungle troops to be out of combat positions as the overall pullout from this war continues.

Thanks for being there before and now and when I return. With any luck, this July 4th will be a special day for me to celebrate our independence. A time with the best family in America. A time to try putting some peaceful sounds back in me. This has been all the excitement and conflict I'll need for a lifetime. Love to Caroline and Jeff. Give old Jake a scratch behind the ear for me. Take it easy. June 15th can't come soon enough for my Army discharge.

Love,
Tom

CONFLICT

PRACTICE THE SKILLS

A. Vocabulary Skills

1. The word **detonated** is associated with (a) weather (b) bombs (c) planes (d) food.

2. Explain the meaning of the word **floor** as used in the selection.

   _____

   _____

3. The word in the selection that means the same as **Independence** is (a) conflict (b) duty (c) pullout (d) freedom.

B. Comprehension Skills

1. Copy a sentence that contains the information to answer the question, **How do you know that Tom is somewhere that he does not like?** _____

   _____

2. Tom is fighting in which war? (a) World War I (b) World War II (c) Korean War (d) Vietnam War

3. Which of the following events are in the proper sequence? (a) central camp, Bien Hoa, May 1, Army discharge (b) Bien Hoa, central camp, May 1, Army discharge (c) May 1, central camp, Army discharge, Bien Hoa (d) Bien Hoa, May 1, central camp, Army discharge

4. The major topic for the minor topics **showers, hot food, rest** is (a) New Year's Eve (b) central camp (c) jungle camp (d) Bien Hoa.

5. The best main idea for the entire selection is
   (a) feelings about war and conflict from a young soldier
   (b) America's history of war in other countries
   (c) the effects of war and conflict on families at home
   (d) how geography affects the outcome of war

6. Contrast Tom's last Fourth of July with the next Fourth of July.

_____

7. Next Tuesday is day twenty is a fact. Which of the following phrases added to the sentence would make it an opinion?   (a) when the helicopter comes   (b) and off to central camp   (c) the safest day of the month   (d) and almost three weeks of jungle living have passed

8. You would guess that Tom's most important possession is a
   (a) letter   (b) firefight   (c) helicopter   (d) gun.

9. Tom's biggest problem is surviving the conflict of war until
   (a) March   (b) May 1   (c) June 15   (d) July 4.

10. The author probably thinks that this war is   (a) unnecessary
   (b) patriotic   (c) enjoyable   (d) necessary.

   Explain your answer in one sentence. _____

_____

C. Study Skills

1. Complete the following outline with information from the selection.

   I. Three types of conflict from the selection
     A. Self against self
       1. I was scared to death

     B. _____

       1. _____

     C. _____

       1. _____

2. Summarize in one or two sentences what Tom needs to do to make it to June 15. _____

_____

D. Writing Skills

1. Write one or two sentences explaining which type of conflict you think is the most difficult for Tom to deal with and give at least two examples for your choice. Use the following format.

I think that self against _____ **is the most difficult**

conflict for Tom because _____

_____

2. Write a letter to Tom either as his father/mother or sister/brother. Include at least four sentences. _____

_____

_____

_____

Unit Activities

Reread each selection carefully and then complete the following activities independently or in cooperative groups.

Connecting the Theme and Selections

1. Know. List one major example of conflict in each selection. The first example is done for you.

The conflict in Selection A involves a girl alone in a house.

The conflict in Selection B involves _____

The conflict in Selection C involves _____

CONFLICT

2. Comprehend. List the major type of conflict for each selection.

The major type of conflict in Selection A is self against _____

The major type of conflict in Selection B is self against _____

The major type of conflict in Selection C is self against _____

3. Apply. Illustrate the conflict shown in one of the selections with a picture or drawing of your own.

4. Analyze. Classify each selection in order of the depth or seriousness of the conflict and give one reason for your choice.

Selection __ is the most serious example of conflict because _____

_____

_____

_____

Selection __ is the second most serious example _____

_____

_____

_____

Selection __ is third because _____

_____

_____

_____

5. Synthesize. Set up a conflict mediation program for the speaker in Selection A or Tom in Selection C. Give three recommendations that would help either deal with the conflict.

Recommendation 1. _____

Recommendation 2. _____

Recommendation 3. _____

6. Evaluate. Predict the outcome of the conflict in each selection. An example is done for you.

Example. In Selection A, the speaker calls the police and they patrol the neighborhood until the parents return home.

In Selection A, _____

In Selection B, _____

In Selection C, _____

Applying the Theme and Selections to the Real World

Use a variety of newspapers, magazines, and other reference materials to complete your choice of the following projects or those assigned to you. Also consider using CD-ROM encyclopedias and other on-line databases as well as television programs and videos to get information for your projects.

Interdisciplinary Project 1

Create a collage of the four types of conflict. Give at least two examples of each type and the way the conflict was mediated or how you would have solved it.

Interdisciplinary Project 2

Choose one of the four types of conflict that you think most people experience and fear the most. Give the type of conflict, three common examples that most of us face daily, three reasons why we fear this type the most, and three ways that dealing with that conflict might be easier. Complete your project in outline form.

Interdisciplinary Project 3

Watch a current movie, read a short story, and read one newspaper article. Take notes about examples of conflict in each. Then complete a report. Explain the examples, the type of conflict for each example, and how the conflict was mediated or solved. Also comment about the reality of the conflict and the solutions presented.

Interdisciplinary Project 4

Watch a television documentary about weather, geography, or disease. Explain examples of self against nature in the program. Also explain how the conflict of self against self is presented.

Interdisciplinary Project 5

Write a one-act play about conflict with one to four characters. Focus on one specific type of conflict within the play's action. Be sure to have the conflict solved in some realistic way.

UNIT 5

The Theme of
DEMOCRACY

Definition

DEMOCRACY is formal or informal government by the people of a country, state, or group in which there are equal rights, opportunities, and treatment for all.

PREREADING ACTIVITY

1. Think about all the times you observe democracy in action.

   a. The election of the president of the country, governor of a state, or local officials
   b. The right to have a high school education and to attend college
   c. The right to start your own business

2. Think about what allows these and other examples of democracy to take place.

   a. The Constitution of the United States and the constitution of each state
   b. Again, guarantees in the Constitution and the number of colleges to choose from
   c. Our democratic system of free enterprise

3. Think about how these examples improve our lives.

   a. Guaranteed opportunities to change elected officials and power in government to prevent dictatorship
   b. An education gives more opportunities for choices in the job market and better-paying jobs to improve your lifestyle
   c. Starting your own business allows you to be more independent and to have more control over decisions

4. Now give two examples of your own of democracy and how each improves the lives of those affected by the democratic actions.

DEMOCRACY

Example 1. A mayor of a city puts funds in the school budget for after-school programs in each school. Students with nothing to do after school can now participate in a variety of programs throughout the school year.

Example 2. _____

_____

Example 3. _____

_____

SELECTION A

    Mrs. Mary Leavitt is retiring from her thirty-year career as a social worker in a big city. She and her husband have raised six children: two doctors, two teachers, a lawyer, and a missionary in Africa. Mrs. Leavitt's coworkers have gathered for a dinner in her honor. After dinner, Mrs. Leavitt's boss makes a brief speech. She praises her work and her dedication to her clients. Then she asks Mrs. Leavitt to say a few words.

    "I believe in the principles of democracy," Mrs. Leavitt begins. "In all my years as a social worker, I have given this simple message to each person I've worked with: 'I can't solve your problems. I can only help you find opportunities for you to help yourself build a better life.'

    "People need to understand that we Americans have rights like no other people on this planet. It is up to each of us to use those rights to make good decisions, to work hard, and to help the 'other guy' when we can.

    "My children always asked me why their father and I

wanted them to make so many decisions. We asked them to help decide about clothes, school, chores, where to vacation, and all sorts of things. Children who grow up making decisions become better decision makers as adults.

"Making decisions is part of living in a democracy. As adults, the decision-making process involves voting, career choices, marriage, where to live, and how to spend money. These decisions are not always easy to make, but we all have to live with the consequences of our decisions.

"I always reminded my children that they had two important choices to make when high school ended: What were they going to do with their lives, and how were they going to pay for it?

"Growing up, my kids learned to appreciate democratic principles—even after living with their two dictators! But look at them today. They show no signs of significant suffering during their childhood years. Opportunities for part-time work, scholarships, and student loans pave the way to success when they are combined with discipline, hard work, and a few clear goals. And now I think my children truly appreciate the values behind democracy.

"Good homes are like good governments. You treat each child and person equally and provide the right to pursue happiness. It's up to each one of us to take it from there.

"I thank you for your friendship, and I will miss you all."

PRACTICE THE SKILLS

A. Vocabulary Skills

1. Mrs. Leavitt's career was in social work. Which one of her children's careers do you think is most associated with **social work**?
(a) doctor   (b) lawyer   (c) teacher   (d) missionary

2. The word **principles** as used in the selection could be replaced with
(a) dictators   (b) basic ideas   (c) careers   (d) decisions.

3. In the phrase **the right to pursue happiness,** the word **pursue** means   (*a*) surrender   (*b*) purchase   (*c*) solve   (*d*) achieve.

B. Comprehension Skills

1. The most information about making decisions is located in which paragraph?   (*a*) first   (*b*) second   (*c*) third   (*d*) fourth

2. According to the selection, **good homes are like good** (*a*) businesses   (*b*) schools   (*c*) governments   (*d*) marriages.

3. What event happens to Mary Leavitt after the events of the selection?   (*a*) marriage   (*b*) law school   (*c*) elected office (*d*) retirement

4. The major topic for the minor topics **part-time work, scholarships, student loans, discipline, hard work, goals** is   (*a*) things that pave the way to success   (*b*) things that exist in all governments (*c*) things that make people happy   (*d*) things to avoid in childhood.

5. The best title for this selection is:
   (*a*) Good Career Opportunities in Social Work
   (*b*) Life After High School
   (*c*) The Principles of Democracy in Everyday Life
   (*d*) Comparing Democracy to Dictatorships

6. Mary Leavitt's success as a parent is probably related to the fact that she   (*a*) made her husband work two jobs   (*b*) taught her children to make decisions   (*c*) taught her children how to make money   (*d*) made her children move out after high school.

7. The sentence **Children who grow up making decisions become better decision makers as adults** is an opinion. Rewrite the sentence into a fact.

_____

_____

8. Which of the following is NOT a democratic principle?   (*a*) making decisions   (*b*) treating people equally   (*c*) pursuing happiness (*d*) becoming a parent

9. It seems that people in a good democracy have good   (*a*) values (*b*) income   (*c*) friends   (*d*) education.

Explain your answer. _____

_____

10. What does the author think about Mary Leavitt?   (*a*) dislikes her (*b*) admires her   (*c*) thinks she is too strict   (*d*) thinks she would make a great doctor or lawyer

C. Study Skills

1. Complete the following outline with information from the selection and with information of your own.

   I. Three principles that Mary Leavitt followed as a social worker

   A. _____

   B. _____
   C. Help the other person when we can
   II. Three principles that Mary Leavitt followed as a parent
   A. Make children make decisions

   B. _____

   C. _____

2. Summarize in two sentences why Mary Leavitt was a good social worker and/or parent. _____

_____

D. Writing Skills

1. Write at least two sentences predicting what Mary Leavitt will do with her time during retirement. _____

_____

_____

_____

2. Pretend that you are one of Mary Leavitt's children and you cannot attend the retirement award evening. Write at least four sentences in a personal letter to her.

_____

_____

_____

_____

 **SELECTION B**

Do you have any idea who decides what you study in school? Who makes the decisions, and how are the decisions reached? Does the school board rule, or the superintendent of schools, or the state Board of Education?

In September, Kingswood Secondary School will open its doors to new students and new programs. For the past three years, students, school staff, parents, members of the community, and business leaders have been meeting together. They have been discussing new ideas for Kingswood, and they have listened carefully to each other's views. They have reached a consensus (agreement) on four new approaches.

First, students in grades six to ten will be grouped

into clusters. There will be about one hundred students in each cluster and two or three clusters per grade. Each cluster will stay together during most of the school day, so students will enjoy the benefits of being in a small school. A team of four teachers (English, social studies, science, and math) will be assigned to each cluster. These teams will have time to plan together lessons and field trips. They will contact parents about the progress of each child.

Second, the school day will change. Kingswood's school day used to have seven fifty-minute periods. This year, the school day will have four or five longer periods 90 to 120 minutes long. (This type of schedule is called block scheduling.) During these longer periods, students will have time to work together in small groups and to complete projects.

Third, teachers will have different goals. They will emphasize reading literature about subjects, doing research, writing reports, completing projects, and using computers. Teachers will also try to integrate (or connect) the three main subjects: humanities (English, social studies, and the arts), math, and science. Although fewer topics will be studied, each topic will be studied in more depth and across different subjects.

For example, a month-long unit in the tenth grade might be about the Civil War. In social studies, students will study the politics of the North and South. They will focus on the presidency of Abraham Lincoln and the outcomes of the war. In English class, students will read *The Red Badge of Courage* and *Uncle Tom's Cabin*, two novels about the war. In music class, they will sing the spirituals sung by slaves.

The fourth new program at Kingswood begins in grade eleven. Students entering grade eleven will choose a "Career Pathway." Their choices will be college preparation, finance, health services, technology, and drafting and engineering. In each pathway, courses will emphasize the relationship of that course to college, careers, and the real world. For example, an American history course for students in the finance pathway might stress the history of

American business. In the health services pathway, the American history course might focus on how health services have changed over the last hundred years.

Students, teachers, administrators, parents, and community members have worked hard to bring about these changes at Kingswood. In the years of planning and decision making, they employed three essential principles of democracy: thorough and open discussion of issues, respect for each other's views, and voting. Their work and the democratic process they used have already improved both the school and the community.

PRACTICE THE SKILLS

A. Vocabulary Skills

1. The word **cluster** as used in the selection is a group of   (a) parents and community people   (b) students and teachers   (c) principals and businessmen   (d) computers and textbooks.

2. The word **block** as used in the selection refers to a   (a) group of people   (b) shape for classrooms   (c) way of voting   (d) period of time.

3. When there is a **consensus,** people reach   (a) a specific place   (b) an argument   (c) an agreement   (d) a disagreement.

B. Comprehension Skills

1. What three subjects are included in the humanities? _____

_____

2. In what grade do the Career Pathways begin?   (a) sixth   (b) tenth   (c) eleventh   (d) college

3. Which event(s) had to happen before the new programs at Kingswood could be announced?   (*a*) The old building was destroyed and a new one was built.   (*b*) Students learned to use computers.   (*c*) Many people discussed the programs and made decisions.   (*d*) All students chose their pathways.

4. Two of the four minor topics for the major topic **curriculum goals** are   (*a*) doing research and writing reports   (*b*) going to college and choosing a career   (*c*) leaving school and starting a job (*d*) organizing a cluster and making a block schedule.

5. The best main idea of this selection is about using democracy to produce better   (*a*) teaching and learning   (*b*) colleges and careers (*c*) science and math courses   (*d*) parents and teachers.

6. Which of the following happens in block scheduling?   (*a*) Class periods are longer.   (*b*) There are fewer class periods in a school day.   (*c*) Students work in small groups.   (*d*) All of these happen.

7. The third paragraph contains facts about clusters. Copy one of the sentences about clusters from this paragraph and rewrite it into an opinion. _____

_____

_____

8. You would guess that a major objective of the new services at Kingswood is to increase   (*a*) after-school programs   (*b*) parent involvement   (*c*) public relations   (*d*) taxes for a new school.

9. The theme of democracy shows at Kingswood through   (*a*) how decisions are made   (*b*) how students are elected to student council (*c*) how the budget is spent   (*d*) how the principal establishes discipline codes.

10. From reading this selection, you can guess that the author believes that   (*a*) public schools need to change   (*b*) the school day needs to be longer   (*c*) business needs to contribute computers to schools (*d*) English and math are the most important subjects.

C. Study Skills

1. Complete the following outline with information from the selection.

I. Three important facts about clusters
   A. About one hundred students each

   B. _____

   C. _____

II. Three important facts about block scheduling

   A. _____

   B. _____

   C. _____

III. Three important facts about curriculum
   A. Emphasis on reading literature, doing research, writing reports

   B. _____

   C. _____

IV. _____
   A. College preparation, finance, health services, technology, drafting

   B. _____

   C. _____

2. Summarize one of the four major changes from the major topics in the outline above. Give one reason why you think it is the most important one. **I think that** _____ **is the most important**

change because _____

_____

D. Writing Skills

1. Write one sentence recommending a change in your school or job. **I**

think that _____ **should change because** _____

_____

2. Pretend that you are the principal of Kingswood Secondary School and you are doing a cable television program to inform the community about the new ways the school will service students. Write the first four sentences of your script.

_____

_____

_____

_____

 SELECTION C

Why do so many people in other countries want to live in the United States? People all over the world envy America's system of government. American democracy has its roots both in our country's history and in its documents.

There are examples of democratic ideas in our country's earliest history. For instance, the Pilgrims came to America in the 1600s so they could be free to practice their own religion. The American colonies were ruled by the British king and Parliament, but the colonists had no representatives in Parliament. The colonies reached a boiling point in 1773 with the Boston Tea Party. Britain had imposed new, high taxes on tea. The colonists objected: There should be "no taxation without representation." A handful of angry colonists dumped a boatload of British tea into Boston's harbor. This small-scale protest was an important event leading to the American Revolution.

Two historic documents define the principles of American democracy: the Declaration of Independence and the United States Constitution.

In 1776, Thomas Jefferson wrote the Declaration of Independence. This document established America's independence from Britain. It also established the thirteen colonies as one country—the United States of America.

Fifty-six members of the Continental Congress signed the Declaration of Independence on July 4, 1776.

Here is the Declaration's second paragraph. Think about how the idea of democracy is woven into these words:

We hold these truths to be self-evident: that all men are created equal, that they are endowed by their Creator with certain unalienable [cannot be taken away] rights, that among these are life, liberty, and the pursuit of happiness.

The Constitution was written after the Revolutionary War. It sets forth the organization and powers of the new federal government. The Constitution was signed on September 17, 1787, and ratified in June of 1788.

Think about the theme of democracy in the Preamble, or introduction, to the Constitution:

We, the people of the United States, in order to form a more perfect union, establish justice, insure domestic tranquility, provide for the common defense, promote the general welfare, and secure the blessings of liberty to ourselves and our posterity, do ordain and establish this Constitution for the United States of America.

The idea of democracy—rule by the people—is the basis of our American government. The people "rule" by voting for elected representatives. People in countries where there is no democracy envy our system of government.

PRACTICE THE SKILLS

A. Vocabulary Skills

1. The phrase **boiling point** as used in the selection refers to (a) water (b) food (c) feelings (d) democracy.

2. In order to have a **revolution,** there has to be   (*a*) a protest and a rebellion   (*b*) democracy and taxes   (*c*) a Preamble and a Constitution   (*d*) a Pilgrim and a British soldier.

3. In the sentence that begins **We hold these truths to be self-evident,** the word **self-evident** means   (*a*) unusual   (*b*) confusing   (*c*) necessary   (*d*) obvious.

B. Comprehension Skills

1. Copy the two sentences that contain the information to answer the following two questions.

What did the Declaration of Independence establish? _____

_____

What did the Constitution establish?_____

_____

2. The American holiday that celebrates the signing of the Declaration of Independence is   (*a*) Martin Luther King Day   (*b*) Presidents' Day   (*c*) Memorial Day   (*d*) July Fourth.

3. Which of the following events DID NOT occur after the Boston Tea Party?   (*a*) the American Revolution   (*b*) the writing of the Declaration of Independence   (*c*) the Pilgrims' arrival to America   (*d*) independence from England

4. The major topic for the minor topics **life, liberty, pursuit of happiness** is   (*a*) rights given to the colonists by the British   (*b*) rights given in the Declaration of Independence   (*c*) rights given in the Bill of Rights   (*d*) rights given in Amendments 11–27.

5. Write your own one-sentence main idea for the entire selection. Begin with **Democracy is** _____

_____

6. What caused the Boston Tea Party?　(*a*) the American Revolution　(*b*) the British surrender　(*c*) "taxation without representation"　(*d*) the breakup of the thirteen colonies

7. Copy one fact about democracy from the selection and rewrite it into an opinion.

_____

_____

8. Which document describes the three branches of the United States federal government?　(*a*) the Declaration of Independence　(*b*) the Constitution　(*c*) the Continental Congress　(*d*) the Parliament

9. In order to preserve democracy in the United States, all of the following are necessary EXCEPT　(*a*) a strong government　(*b*) a strong defense　(*c*) a strong justice system　(*d*) a strong relationship with foreign countries.

10. Why did the author write this selection? _____

_____

C. Study Skills

1. Complete the following outline with information from the selection.

  I. Three important facts about the Declaration of Independence

    A. _____

    B. _____

    C. _____

  II. Three important facts about the United States Constitution

    A. _____

    B. _____

    C. _____

2. Summarize why we need the Declaration of Independence and the Constitution. **These two documents are necessary because** _____

_____

_____

_____

D. Writing Skills

1. Write three sentences about democracy in your life by using the same format three times.

   1. **Democracy is important in my life because it allows me to**

     _____

   2. _____

     _____

   3. _____

     _____

2. Write a diary entry of at least four sentences for July 4, 1776, or September 17, 1787, pretending that you are one of the signers of the Declaration of Independence or the Constitution. Begin with the following.

What a great day it is in American history. _____

_____

_____

_____

_____

_____

Unit Activities

Reread each selection carefully and then complete the following activities independently or in cooperative groups.

Connecting the Theme and Selections

1. **Know.** Tell how democracy is shown in each selection. Use the following format.

   Democracy is shown in Selection A through Mary Leavitt's actions as a social worker and a parent.

   Democracy is shown in Selection B through _____

   _____

   _____

   Democracy is shown in Selection C through _____

   _____

   _____

2. **Comprehend.** Explain which selection shows democracy affecting the most people. Give at least two reasons for your choice.

3. **Apply.** Apply one example of democracy from your own life to each selection.

   Selection A. An example of democracy in my job or home is _____

   _____

   Selection B. An example of democracy in my school is _____

   _____

   Selection C. An example of democracy in my country is _____

   _____

4. **Analyze.** List three observations that you have made that seem to contradict the theme of democracy. Then give a reason why you think that situation exists. An example is done for you.

Example. We have equal rights, but there has never been a woman president. A woman has the right to run for president, but our country is not ready to elect its first woman president.

Observation 1. _____

_____

Observation 2. _____

_____

Observation 3. _____

_____

5. **Synthesize.** Imagine that Mary Leavitt is running for president. Write her announcement speech in three or four sentences using the word *democracy* several times.

6. **Evaluate.** Predict three problems that will need attention at the Kingswood Secondary School in the first few months of the new school year. After each problem, give a realistic solution for that problem. An example is done for you.

Example. Students are not reading at the same level of ability. A solution is the teachers will provide an extra period of reading help each day for needy students.

Problem 1. _____

_____

Problem 2. _____

_____

Problem 3. _____

_____

Applying the Theme and Selections to the Real World

Use a variety of newspapers, magazines, and other reference materials to complete your choice of the following projects or those assigned to you. Also consider using CD-ROM encyclopedias and other on-line databases as well as television programs and videos to get information for your projects.

Interdisciplinary Project 1

Research the United Nations. Write a report telling when it was begun, why it was begun, and its most important objectives in terms of democracy.

Interdisciplinary Project 2

Research the four parts of the Declaration of Independence and the four parts of the Constitution. Create a collage of eight pictures or your own drawings, showing a sample of the rights given in each part.

Interdisciplinary Project 3

Choose a current newsmagazine. Find one good example of a country trying to become a democracy. Write a report that explains the progress the country has made and some of the problems it is facing. Illustrate your report.

Interdisciplinary Project 4

Create a ten-minute oral history of democracy in America on audio- or videotape. Include a short discussion of the important events from 1620 to the present.

Interdisciplinary Project 5

Create a college titled "Everyday Democracy." Show ten pictures of simple events or situations that show democracy in everyday life. Focus on the rights given in the Declaration of Rights in the Declaration of Independence and the Preamble to the Constitution.

UNIT 6

The Theme of
DEVOTION

Definition

DEVOTION is the deep and consistent commitment to a person, cause, or career.

PREREADING ACTIVITY

1. Think about people you have seen who are deeply committed to a person, cause, or career.

    a. A mother or father
    b. A member of the clergy or a famous American leader
    c. A teacher or a coach

2. Think of the reasons and the actions that show these people's devotion to a cause or career.

    a. A mother or father's care and affection for a child
    b. A clergy member's depth of belief and dedication to the church or a leader's lifetime spent on issues affecting a country
    c. A teacher's long hours of instruction during and after school or a coach's work on the practice field

3. Now give two examples of your own of devotion that you see other people doing and the reason for the devotion.

> **A first example is done for you.**

Example 1. An animal activist spends his or her life trying to save an endangered species, such as the tiger, from becoming extinct.

Example 2. _____

_____

Example 3. _____

_____

SELECTION A

Usually, I am hesitant to write about my personal life because the experiences are so precious. But perhaps this story will be of some value to others.

I met my husband more than twenty years ago at my older brother's funeral. It was the darkest time of my life. My brother had been out jogging when he was struck and killed by a drunk driver.

Someone called my brother's close friends. Within several hours of being called, John, a friend of my brother's, arrived to express his sympathies. I had never met John before but knew of him from my brother's army days. My brother would often remind me—by mail, by phone, and in person—that he had found the perfect husband for me.

Somehow—perhaps it was fate—I was the one assigned to meet John at the airport. We both sensed something special right away. It was a feeling that comes in the darkest hours of grief and sadness but can also be the start of something wonderful for a lifetime.

Three days later the courtship began, and two years later we were married. Those two years were filled with respect and kindness. The two words *respect* and *kindness* have an even deeper meaning now—twenty years later. I can honestly say that we treasure our marriage even more today than at any time to this moment.

I hope some young man or young woman reads this and chooses to put devotion into a relationship and build a life on that strong emotion.

PRACTICE THE SKILLS

A. Vocabulary Skills

1. In the first sentence of the selection, the word **precious** means (*a*) forgetful (*b*) unfortunate (*c*) valuable (*d*) distant.

2. In the sentence beginning, **Three days later the courtship began,** the word **courtship** is replaced best with   (*a*) dating (*b*) employment   (*c*) marriage   (*d*) vacation.

3. The word **treasure** as used in the selection refers to   (*a*) pirates (*b*) money   (*c*) prizes   (*d*) feelings.

B.   Comprehension Skills

1. Copy the phrase or sentence that answers the question, **Where did the woman first meet her husband?** _____

_____

2. How was the narrator's brother killed?   (*a*) war   (*b*) drunk driver (*c*) plane crash   (*d*) heart attack

3. Which of the following DID NOT happen after the narrator's brother was killed?   (*a*) Friends were contacted.   (*b*) John arrived.   (*c*) The narrator joined the army.   (*d*) The courtship began.

4. The best major topic for **by mail, by phone,** and **in person** according to the selection is   (*a*) how the friends were contacted (*b*) how the narrator communicated with her future husband (*c*) how the word spread about the brother's death   (*d*) how the brother reminded his sister about the perfect husband.

5. The best title for this whole selection is   (*a*) Brother's Death Brings Much Sadness   (*b*) Enforce Drunk-Driving Laws   (*c*) True Love Grows and Grows   (*d*) Successful Dating Tips.

6. How would you describe the marriage in the selection after twenty years?   (*a*) improving   (*b*) failing   (*c*) about the same   (*d*) ended

7. In the following two sentences from the selection, which one is a fact and which one is an opinion? **I met my husband more than twenty years ago at my older brother's funeral. It was the darkest time of my life.** _____

_____

8. How would you describe the general health of the narrator's brother before he was killed? Explain your answer. _____

_____

9. According to the author, which of the following sets of words best contributes to a successful relationship such as a marriage? (*a*) wealth, contact, sympathy   (*b*) respect, kindness, devotion (*c*) courtship, emotion, fate   (*d*) devotion, wealth, sadness

10. Copy one sentence from the selection that explains why the author wrote this selection. _____

_____

C. Study Skills

1. Complete the following outline of events from the selection.

   I. Five major events that happened after the brother was killed

   A. _____

   B. _____

   C. _____

   D. _____
   E. Married two years later

2. Summarize the entire selection by completing the following sentence.

   The entire selection is about _____

_____

D. Writing Skills

1. Add another sentence to end the selection by completing the following. **I also hope** _____

_____

2. Pretend that you are the narrator. Write a diary entry for the day you went to the airport to meet John for the first time. Or write the diary entry John might have written that same day. _____

_____

_____

_____

_____

SELECTION B

If a smile is the shortest distance between two people, then Dr. William Umansky has made the world a lot smaller. Dr. Umansky is a plastic surgeon in southern California. (A plastic surgeon does operations that improve a patient's appearance.) Dr. Umansky spends most of his time doing surgery on patients who have been disfigured by accidents or birth defects.

Once a year, Dr. Umansky takes his devotion to medicine and people to another level. For about two weeks every year, Dr. Umansky becomes a medical philanthropist (someone who is devoted to helping others). He joins a team of medical experts, and they travel to a remote part of the world. There they give their talents free of charge to help people—especially children—who need medical services.

In El Salvador recently, the team focused on deformities in poor children. Dr. Umansky and a team of nine doctors and nurses performed fifty operations on forty-four children in just nine days. Most of the operations repaired cleft lips and cleft palates. (The palate is the roof of the mouth.) These birth defects disfigure the mouth and face. They also prevent children from speaking and smiling normally.

Both of these birth defects are much more common in Central America than in the United States. In Central

America, they occur in about 1 out of 350 births, compared with 1 out of 1,000 in the United States. Dr. Umansky believes that the primary causes of these birth defects are prenatal stress, poor nutrition, and various legal and illegal drugs consumed by the pregnant woman.

Dr. Umansky and his team could spend their free time on themselves, relaxing with their families. Instead, these caring doctors and nurses devote their skills, their time, and their energy to helping needy people without access to medical care. In Peru, Bangladesh, and Mexico, Dr. Umansky and his team have brought smiles to the faces of all their patients.

PRACTICE THE SKILLS

A. Vocabulary Skills

1. Copy the definition of a **philanthropist** from the selection and then use it in a new sentence of your own. _____

_____

_____

2. In the phrase **remote part of the world,** the word **remote** could be replaced with   (a) modern   (b) undeveloped   (c) wealthy   (d) sickly.

3. Write a word of your own that means the same as **consumed** as used in the selection. _____

B. Comprehension Skills

1. Which paragraph contains information related to where Dr. Umansky and the team went and the number and types of operations they performed?   (a) second   (b) third   (c) fourth   (d) fifth

2. Where does Dr. Umansky live for most of the year?   (a) California   (b) El Salvador   (c) Peru   (d) Mexico

3. Children with cleft lips and cleft palates develop such defects
(*a*) before birth   (*b*) during birth   (*c*) after birth   (*d*) in accidents.

4. The best major topic for the minor topics **Peru, Bangladesh,** and
Mexico is   (*a*) countries of Central America   (*b*) cities in southern
California   (*c*) countries where Dr. Umansky has done operations
(*d*) countries with low numbers of birth defects.

5. The best main idea for the selection is   (*a*) doctor devotes time and
talents to help needy children in other countries   (*b*) doctor devotes
lifetime to children of Central America   (*c*) doctor devotes life to
plastic surgery   (*d*) doctor devotes time for children of California.

6. Which of the following is NOT a cause of birth defects according to
Dr. Umansky?   (*a*) stress   (*b*) weather   (*c*) diet   (*d*) drugs

7. Does the following sentence present facts or opinions? **In Central
America, they occur in about 1 out of 350 births, compared
with 1 out of 1,000 in the United States.** _____

8. Based on the information in the sentence in question 7, you would
conclude that there are   (*a*) more birth defects in the United States
than Central America   (*b*) fewer birth defects in the United States
than Central America   (*c*) about the same number of birth defects in
the United States and Central America   (*d*) no birth defects in the
United States.

Explain your answer. _____

_____

9. You would reason that Dr. Umansky would help more people in
other countries if he had more   (*a*) skills   (*b*) equipment   (*c*) time
(*d*) patients.

10. The author's purpose in writing this selection is to give
(*a*) entertainment   (*b*) opinions   (*c*) instructions   (*d*) information.

C. Study Skills

1. Complete the following outline with information from the selection.

    I. Information about cleft lips and cleft palates
       A. They are birth defects

       B. _____

       C. _____

       D. _____

       E. _____

   II. Primary causes of these birth defects

       A. _____

       B. _____

       C. _____

2. Summarize who Dr. Umansky is in one sentence beginning **Dr. Umansky is a doctor who** _____

D. Writing Skills

1. Rewrite the first sentence of the selection into a new sentence of your own.

_____

_____

2. Pretend that you are the leader of a remote country. Write a business letter to Dr. Umansky inviting him to your country to help children in need. Write at least four sentences. _____

_____

_____

_____

 **SELECTION C**

In his last sermon, Dr. Martin Luther King, Jr., described the funeral he would like to have. He didn't want it to be long, he said, and he didn't want anyone to mention his many awards.

I'd like someone to mention that day that Martin Luther King, Jr., tried to give his life serving others. . . . And I want you to say that I tried to love and serve humanity.

Dr. Martin Luther King, Jr., devoted his life to ending racial segregation. He was a Baptist minister in Montgomery, Alabama. In December 1955, he was asked to lead a protest against racial segregation on the city's buses. King believed in using nonviolent methods to bring about change. He organized the African-American citizens of Montgomery to boycott (stop using) the city's buses. The boycott lasted almost a year. When the United States Supreme Court declared that bus segregation was unconstitutional, the boycott ended.

Dr. King became an important national leader. He helped organize sit-ins and marches. He eloquently protested racial injustice. In his famous "I have a dream speech" in Washington, D.C., on August 28, 1963, he proclaimed:

I have a dream that my four little children will one day live in a nation where they will not be judged by the color of their skin but by the content of their character.

In 1964, Dr. King won the Nobel Peace Prize. He wrote five books about nonviolence and social justice. Perhaps his greatest accomplishments, however, are the national civil rights laws. Thanks to the efforts of President Lyndon Johnson and Dr. King, these three important bills became law:

- The Civil Rights Act of 1964 prohibits racial discrimination in public places. It also provides equal opportunity in employment and education for all.
- The Voting Rights Act of 1965 ends barriers to voting. In states where African Americans had been denied the right to vote, federal workers were put in charge of registering new voters.
- The Civil Rights Act of 1968 is also called the Fair Housing Act. It prohibits racial discrimination in the sale and rental of housing.

Dr. King also worked to fight against poverty. As the Vietnam War escalated, he spoke out against the war. Many Americans joined the antiwar movement.

In April 4, 1968, Dr. Martin Luther King, Jr., was assassinated as he stood on the balcony of a motel in Memphis, Tennessee. He was only thirty-nine. His work had brought about great changes, and the changes happened peacefully, as he had hoped they would.

PRACTICE THE SKILLS

A. Vocabulary Skills

1. **In his speeches and writing, he eloquently protested racial injustice.** In this sentence, the word **eloquently** means (*a*) the graceful, powerful use of words (*b*) the use of nonviolent means (*c*) doing something in an angry manner (*d*) doing something you don't want to do.

2. Which word means the same as **prohibits**? (*a*) remains (*b*) begins (*c*) provides (*d*) forbids

3. Someone who is **assassinated** is _____

What context clues helped you figure out the meaning of this word?

_____

B. Comprehension Skills

1. What was Dr. King's regular job before he became involved in the civil rights movement? _____

2. In what city and state did the bus boycott begin? _____
_____ What ended the boycott? _____
_____

3. Write a time line. Tell one important event that happened in each of these years:

1955 _____

1963 _____

1964 _____

1968 _____

4. What is a good major topic for the minor topics **Civil Rights Act of 1964, Voting Rights Act of 1965, Civil Rights Act of 1968**?
_____

5. Write a one-sentence main idea of your own for this selection.
_____
_____

6. In your own words, explain the idea of nonviolent protest. Give two examples. _____
_____
_____
_____

7. How would you describe this selection?   (*a*) mostly facts   (*b*) mostly opinions   (*c*) about the same number of facts and opinions

Explain your answer. _____

_____

8. According to Dr. King's own words, he wanted people to remember him as someone who   (*a*) won the Nobel Prize   (*b*) accepted the old ways   (*c*) wrote five books   (*d*) loved and served humanity.

9. After the civil rights bills were passed, what two movements did Dr. King support? _____

_____

10. The author's main purpose is to   (*a*) amuse the reader (*b*) persuade the reader to take an action   (*c*) give information (*d*) express an opinion.

C. Study Skills

1. Complete the following outline with specific information from the selection.

 I. Civil Rights Acts passed during the 1960s and the meaning of each
   A. 1964—Civil Rights Act—prohibited racial discrimination in public places; provided equal opportunity for jobs and education

   B. _____

   _____

   C. _____

   _____

2. In three or four sentences, summarize Dr. King's accomplishments described in this selection. Cover the years 1955 to 1968.

_____

_____

_____

_____

_____

D. Writing Skills

1. Imagine that Dr. King is alive today. What problems do you think would trouble him? How do you think he might try to solve these problems? Write three or four sentences.

_____

_____

_____

_____

_____

2. How would _you_ go about trying to solve one of the problems you mentioned in the preceding question? Give specific suggestions. Write a four- to seven-sentence paragraph.

_____

_____

_____

_____

_____

_____

Unit Activities

Reread each selection carefully and then complete the following activities independently or in cooperative groups.

Connecting the Theme and Selections

1. **Know.** Recall the main person in each selection and give two examples of what that person was devoted to. An example is done for you.

   In Selection A, the wife was devoted to her husband and her marriage.

   In Selection B, _____

   In Selection C, _____

2. **Comprehend.** Review the three main persons and choose which one has had the most impact on the most people. Give three reasons in outline form.

   I. My choice is _____ for the following reasons

   　　A. _____

   　　B. _____

   　　C. _____

3. **Apply.** Illustrate a scene from each selection in a collage of three drawings of your own or three pictures from other sources.

4. **Analyze.** Rank the three main persons from the selections 1, 2, 3, according to the level of devotion shown. Give at least two reasons for your first choice. Present your entire answer in one paragraph.

5. **Synthesize.** Imagine that you could know one of these three people. Describe your choice and what you would have to do to show equal devotion in order to keep the relationship strong.

6. Evaluate. Predict who or what you will be devoted to at some point in the future. Give specific information in paragraph form with at least four sentences.

Applying the Theme and Selection to the Real World

Use a variety of newspapers, magazines, and other reference materials to complete your choice of the following projects or those assigned to you. Also consider using CD-ROM encyclopedias and other on-line databases as well as television programs and videos to get information for your projects.

Interdisciplinary Project 1

Research three people in American history up to the present who show devotion, with examples from each one's life. Choose one person who was devoted to another person or small group of people, one who was devoted to a cause or a career, and one who was devoted to his or her community or country. Organize your answer in at least one paragraph for each choice.

Interdisciplinary Project 2

Create a poem for each selection. Try to use a variety of poetic forms with some rhyming. Use the word *devotion* at least once in each poem.

Interdisciplinary Project 3

Choose a movie or television program that shows the theme of devotion and explain how the theme is developed. Organize your answer in at least two paragraphs. Describe the events of the movie or program in the first paragraph and how the theme of devotion is shown in the second paragraph.

157

Interdisciplinary Project 4

Use a tape recorder to interview someone you think demonstrates the theme of devotion. Prepare several questions that relate to the theme.

Interdisciplinary Project 5

Create a collage of five pictures from newspapers and magazines that show the theme of devotion. Rank them in order of impact on the most people.

UNIT 7

The Theme of DIVERSITY

Definition

DIVERSITY is people of different backgrounds working together for a common goal. Diversity is a strength and a positive force needed to get things done in school, society, business, athletics, etc.

PREREADING ACTIVITY

1. Think about times you have seen different people working together to accomplish a job or a common goal.

   a. Students learning from teachers in the classroom
   b. Athletes participating and competing in sports events
   c. A group of office workers in a bank learning how to use a new computer system to record checks or deposits

2. Think of the diversity or the differences that these people bring to each example.

   a. The variety of education backgrounds of teachers and the interest levels of students
   b. The different cultural backgrounds and playing abilities of athletes on a sports team as well as the participation of men and women on the same team
   c. Different ages, races, ethnic backgrounds

3. Now give two examples of your own of diversity that you have seen or done.

> **A first example is provided.**

Example 1. A neighborhood of families with different cultural and religious backgrounds conducts a fund-raising drive to help a family repair a fire-damaged home.

Example 2. _____

_____

Example 3. _____

_____

161

SELECTION A

Miguel Flores tells everyone that he must be the happiest man in the world. Miguel has just changed jobs. After four years as a dishwasher, he has been promoted to second cook. Miguel works at the New Age Restaurant and Emporium on the north side of Chicago. Some of his fellow employees grew up in Chicago, but many are from other countries. Miguel is from El Salvador, Anna Tretiak is from Russia, and Mario Barros is from Cuba.

Jackie LaFauci, the restaurant's owner, set out to hire a comfortable mix of workers. New Age is LaFauci's second successful business venture, and every day she receives applications from people looking for jobs. Diversity—differences—is part of her vision for her restaurant.

LaFauci treats her employees well. They receive good wages and other benefits. For example, LaFauci gives her employees time off to attend English classes and basic business courses. The entire workforce meets once a month to discuss how to improve the business. They talk about employee morale, customer service, and investment of profits. All employees have equal input in making decisions.

LaFauci was very impressed with Miguel's recent recommendations. He suggested a free meal for each child who is accompanied by an adult on weekdays. He also suggested a free meal for a customer who dines at the New Age on his or her birthday. Anna Tretiak's input about a profit-sharing plan has been part of LaFauci's benefit plan for the past six years. Each of LaFauci's forty-five employees receives a share of the restaurant's profits.

In Chicago and throughout the state, the two New Age Restaurants have been cited for their diverse workforce and the productivity of their employees. Jackie LaFauci has also been honored for the way she treats her employees. She is a good example of a business leader for the twenty-first century.

PRACTICE THE SKILLS

A. Vocabulary Skills

1. Use the word **promoted** in a sentence of your own. _____

_____

_____

2. An **immigrant** is a person who (*a*) comes to America (*b*) leaves America (*c*) is born in America (*d*) invests in business in America.

3. In the selection, which pair of words has the same meaning? (*a*) classes and workplace (*b*) recommendations and input (*c*) workers and owner (*d*) profit and morale

B. Comprehension Skills

1. Copy the sentences that answer the question, **What recommendations did Miguel make to improve the business?**

_____

_____

2. What three countries do Flores, Tretiak, and Barros come from?

_____

_____

3. When did Miguel Flores become a second cook at the New Age? (*a*) before he came to America (*b*) before the second restaurant opened (*c*) after four years as a dishwasher (*d*) after LaFauci was honored

4. What is the best major topic for the minor topics **profit sharing plan, good wages, English classes**? (*a*) benefits (*b*) businesses (*c*) applications (*d*) recommendations

163

5. The best title for this selection is

    (*a*) New Workers Needed for New Restaurant
    (*b*) Profits Increase in Restaurant Business
    (*c*) Chicago Restaurants Best in America
    (*d*) Chicago Woman Develops New Business Ideas

6. What was the effect of Anna Tretiak's recommended profit-sharing plan?   (*a*) She was promoted.   (*b*) She was cited throughout Illinois. (*c*) It became a benefit for all workers.   (*d*) It gave equal input to other workers.

7. Describe the first two sentences in the selection.   (*a*) fact and fact (*b*) fact and opinion   (*c*) opinion and fact   (*d*) opinion and opinion

    Explain your answer. _____

    _____

8. The New Age Restaurant and Emporium owner   (*a*) serves only Mexican food   (*b*) hires five new workers every day   (*c*) runs a successful adult education program   (*d*) uses new methods of management.

9. You would think that LaFauci is   (*a*) difficult to work for (*b*) respected by her employees   (*c*) known around the country (*d*) interested in owning the most restaurants in Chicago.

10. From this selection, you can guess that the writer favors (*a*) diversity in the workplace   (*b*) college for everyone   (*c*) labor unions for all employees   (*d*) a four-day work week.

C. Study Skills

1. Use information from the selection to complete the following outline.

    I. Immigrant employees at the New Age
      A. Miguel Flores from El Salvador

      B. _____

      C. _____

II. Benefits of working at the New Age

    A. _____

    B. _____

    C. _____

III. Monthly topics of discussion at the New Age

    A. Morale

    B. _____

    C. _____

IV. Recommendations by employees to improve the New Age

    A. _____

    B. _____

    C. _____

2. Complete the following summary with at least two sentences of your own. **Jackie LaFauci is cited locally and throughout Illinois because** _____

_____

_____

_____

D. Writing Skills

1. Write one sentence using information from the selection that contains the 5W's: who, what, when, where, why. A sample is provided. **Anna Tretiak works at the New Age every day because it has good benefits.** _____

_____

2. Write a business letter of at least four sentences to Jackie LaFauci. Ask for a job application to work at the New Age Restaurant and Emporium and give reasons why you want to work there.

_____

_____

_____

_____

_____

 SELECTION B

Travel north from Boston on Interstate 93 and look for the exits for Somerville. Somerville is a city rich in history and in diversity. It is the home of the Highlanders, the nickname of the sports teams of Somerville High School. In 1995 at Somerville High, sports and diversity merged on the soccer field.

That year, Somerville's soccer team, coached by John Chiesa, was a United Nations of players. The team captured the hearts and admiration of not only the whole community but also of cities throughout Massachusetts.

Most of the players had moved to Somerville within the past year or two. They had never played together as a team. Most of them had never attended the same school or even lived in the same country, state, or city. They spoke seven different languages and represented nine different countries. Three were Americans from birth. Seven were from El Salvador. Two were from Cape Verde, a nation of islands off the western coast of Africa. Two were from Brazil, and two were from Guatemala. Two were from Portugal and two from Haiti. Finally, one player was from India and one from Somalia in eastern Africa. The team was a media event unto itself.

DIVERSITY

Somerville's soccer team had four captains that year. Wilmer Ventura and Jimmy Gusman were from El Salvador, Bruno Marques was from Portugal, and Ebbie Kodiat was from India. As the memorable season evolved, the team that didn't wear the same footwear won their league championship with a record of seventeen wins and three losses. Then they were off to the Massachusetts North playoffs, where they won the preliminary game, the quarter-final game, and the semifinal game. Next up was the Massachusetts North final game. That's right, another victory. The Eastern Massachusetts championship game would be the last thrilling victory for this unique team.

Thousands watched the Highlanders play the Massachusetts state championship finals. Before that game, however, Somerville's mayor, city officials, and business owners made sure all those feet were wearing brand-new astroturf shoes. The team had never played on artificial turf, and they certainly had never thought of soccer in the snow. But a freak snowfall proved difficult for both teams. The Highlanders lost the state championship by a score of 3–1.

What a season, and what a lesson in the definition of the word *team*. In Somerville High's lobby are trophies won by that great group of athletes in their incredible 1995 season. They were just a group of young men who came together from around the world one September—and became champions three months later.

PRACTICE THE SKILLS

A. Vocabulary Skills

1. The word **merged** as used in the phrase **sports and diversity merged on the soccer field** means   (*a*) divided   (*b*) came together   (*c*) advertised   (*d*) injured.

2. Which of the following is NOT an example of a **media event**?
(*a*) television interviews with team members   (*b*) newspaper articles about the team   (*c*) cable TV game schedules   (*d*) announcements of winning scores by the principal

3. Evolved as used in the phrase **as the memorable season evolved** refers to   (*a*) time   (*b*) money   (*c*) skills   (*d*) coaching.

B. Comprehension Skills

1. Copy one sentence that answers a question about the native

countries of the players. _____

_____

2. What are the respective numbers relating to languages spoken and countries represented by the players on the team?   (*a*) three and seven   (*b*) two and two   (*c*) seven and nine   (*d*) seven and two

3. Complete the following time line by arranging the events in the order in which they happened. For each event, tell whether the 1995 Somerville soccer team WON or LOST. The first two have been done for you.

- Massachusetts North final game
- League championship
- Massachusetts state championship game
- Eastern Massachusetts championship game
- Playoffs for Massachusetts North

a. League championship—WON
b. Playoffs for Massachusetts North—WON

c. _____

d. _____

e. _____

168

DIVERSITY

4. The best major topic for the minor topics **El Salvador, Portugal, India** is   (*a*) countries representing the most players   (*b*) countries representing the most languages spoken   (*c*) countries of the captains   (*d*) countries without team representatives.

5. Which of the following main ideas best relates to this selection?
(*a*) Soccer team shows value of diversity.
(*b*) Soccer team wins state championship.
(*c*) Soccer team visits United Nations.
(*d*) Soccer team and coach shown on television.

6. The Somerville soccer team members differed most in
(*a*) backgrounds   (*b*) soccer ability   (*c*) grades in school   (*d*) ages.

7. Reread the first sentence of the selection. Which of the following rewritten sentences is a pure fact?
(*a*) Somerville is a city rich in history and diversity.
(*b*) Somerville is located in the best area near Boston.
(*c*) Somerville is the easiest city to get to off Interstate 93.
(*d*) Somerville is located near Boston off Interstate 93.

8. Use your imagination to think of two reasons why the city officials

and business owners bought the team new shoes. _____

_____

_____

_____

9. From reading this selection, you can guess that the city of Somerville, Massachusetts, has   (*a*) overcrowded schools   (*b*) a large immigrant population   (*c*) a population of about 100,000   (*d*) traffic problems like Boston.

10. The author's purpose in writing this selection was probably to
(*a*) promote soccer   (*b*) give an example of diversity   (*c*) give credit to a great coach   (*d*) encourage a trip to the United Nations.

C. Study Skills

1. Complete the following outline with information from the selection.

   I. Number of players and countries shown on the team
      A. Three from America

      B. _____

      C. _____

      D. _____

      E. _____

      F. _____

      G. _____

      H. _____

      I. _____

  II. Team captains and home countries
      A. Wilmer Ventura and Jimmy Gusman from El Salvador

      B. _____

      C. _____

2. Summarize the Massachusetts state championship game in one complete sentence. _____

_____

D. Writing Skills

1. Copy the sentence from the selection that you think best shows the theme of diversity. _____

_____

Explain the reason for your choice in one sentence of your own.

_____

2. Imagine that you are a newspaper or television reporter. The Highlanders soccer team has just lost the state championship game. Write at least four sentences describing their 1995 season.

_____

_____

_____

_____

 SELECTION C

What do you think would happen if everyone were exactly like everyone else? Would the business world be better or worse?

The world of work and business is a dynamic and always changing environment. Situations change, people change—nothing stays exactly the same all the time. If American businesses are to be successful into the twenty-first century, experts tell us, they need to broaden their workforce. This means having a variety of employees who differ in race, gender, age, and culture.

To help bring about that goal, the Equal Employment Opportunity Commission was created in 1964. This federal agency is often referred to as the EEOC. Its purpose is to make sure that everyone—regardless of race, religion, gender, and country of origin—has an equal chance to apply for jobs. If you look carefully at want ads, you will see that many businesses identify themselves as "an EEO company."

Economists (business experts), sociologists (experts who study people and groups), and teachers tell us that some groups are more effective than others. When people with diverse backgrounds join a group, they bring different knowledge and experiences to the group. They are also likely to have different approaches to solving problems.

171

Such a diverse group is more effective than a group of workers who are homogeneous—all alike.

The process of change requires that people be flexible in their attitudes. They must be able to exchange ideas and use skills so that they can work together to accomplish the group's goals.

Recently a company made the following statements in support of diversity in both school and business.

- Diversity brings new energy and creativity to school and the workplace.
- Diversity in school and the workplace results in better problem solving.
- Diversity in school and the workplace can nurture tolerance of diversity in society.
- Diversity in school and the workplace helps people become more aware of the needs of the outside world.
- Diversity strengthens the management of school and the workplace.

Do you agree or disagree with these statements about diversity? Think about your own experiences. Can you give an example to support each statement?

PRACTICE THE SKILLS

A. Vocabulary Skills

1. In the first sentence of the second paragraph, the best context clue that means almost the same as **dynamic** is (*a*) world (*b*) business (*c*) changing (*d*) environment.

2. In the phrase **they need to broaden their workforce,** the word **broaden** means (*a*) reduce (*b*) expand (*c*) educate (*d*) punish.

3. Rewrite the following sentence by replacing the phrase **nurture tolerance** with new words of your own. **Diversity in school and the workplace can nurture tolerance of diversity in society.**

_____

_____

B. Comprehension Skills

1. What is the purpose of the Equal Employment Opportunity

Commission? _____

_____

_____

2. Which of the following groups is NOT mentioned in the selection? (*a*) business experts (*b*) American businesses (*c*) American schools (*d*) sports teams

3. Experts agree that to be most effective, (*a*) group members need to be alike (*b*) groups should be made up of members with different backgrounds (*c*) groups need to follow orders exactly (*d*) people should work alone and not in groups.

4. List at least two minor topics from the selection for the major topic

people who understand how to achieve goals. _____

_____

5. Use the three words **century, diversity, goals** and write a one-

sentence main idea of your own for the entire selection. _____

_____

DIVERSITY

6. You would guess that the major difference between a successful company and an unsuccessful company is   (*a*) how many educated workers it hires   (*b*) how well it uses people's skills   (*c*) how well it avoids EEOC laws   (*d*) how well it pays its workers.

7. Would most people argue that the third and fourth sentences of the second paragraph are both facts or both opinions? Explain your answer.

_____

_____

_____

8. What is meant by the expression **the whole is more important than the individual parts**? _____

_____

Give an example from your own experiences. _____

_____

_____

_____

9. Where are most businesses concerned about developing an awareness and understanding of diversity?   (*a*) in schools   (*b*) in families   (*c*) in neighborhoods   (*d*) in law firms and banks

Why? _____

_____

10. The author's purpose in writing this selection is to   (*a*) entertain   (*b*) inform   (*c*) suggest new careers   (*d*) give lessons.

Explain your answer. _____

_____

DIVERSITY

C. Study Skills

1. Complete the following outline with information from the selection and information of your own.

    I. Ten things I learned about diversity
      A. First, I learned that diversity can mean race, gender, age, or culture
      B. I learned that there are laws to provide equal access to jobs
      C. I learned that American business needs to make changes in its workforce

      D. I learned _____

      E. _____

      F. _____

      G. _____

      H. _____

      I. _____

      J. _____

2. Complete the following sentence. **In order to have a successful business, you** _____

D. Writing Skills

1. Write one sentence of your own that could be added to the list of recommendations offered by the company. Begin your sentence with the word **Diversity.**

_____

_____

_____

2. Write at least four sentences that would be the introductory paragraph of a booklet about your company and its purpose and/or values regarding diversity. Introduce our paragraph with the following. **Our company wants workers who have different**

backgrounds and experiences. _____

_____

_____

_____

_____

_____

Unit Activities

Reread each selection carefully and then complete the following activities independently or in cooperative groups.

Connecting the Theme and Selections

1. Know. Identify how diversity shows in each selection.
Diversity shows in the restaurant business in Selection A.

_____ in Selection B.

_____ In Selection C.

2. Comprehend. Compare the roles of Jackie LaFauci in Selection A and John Chiesa in Selection B regarding the theme of diversity.

3. Apply. Illustrate in a drawing or in a paragraph a problem that LaFauci and Chiesa might have regarding diversity. Then use information from Selection C to explain why the problem needs to be solved.

DIVERSITY

4. **Analyze.** List the recommendations offered by the company in Selection C. Then choose an example or make up your own from Selection A and B to support each recommendation. The format and an example are given.

Example 1. Diversity brings new energy and creativity to school and the workplace.
Selection A. Different workers gave new ideas to increase profits.
Selection B. The soccer team showed more energy as the season moved along.

Example 2. _____

Selection A. _____

Selection B. _____

Example 3. _____

Selection A. _____

Selection B. _____

Example 4. _____

Selection A. _____

Selection B. _____

Example 5. _____

Selection A. _____

Selection B. _____

5. **Synthesize.** Design the third New Age Restaurant and Emporium. Tell about two new employees and their jobs, some new ideas to increase profits, some benefits, and so on. Try to put your information in the following form. A first example is done for you.

   I. New Age Restaurant #3

      A. New employee: Adalino Cabral from Portgual is the new office manager. He wants to increase profits by making a New Age coupon book as a gift-giving idea. The book will contain special discounts and free meals on certain dates. He wants to offer a benefit of a college savings plan for employees or their children.

DIVERSITY

B. New employee: _____

_____

_____

_____

C. New employee: _____

_____

_____

_____

6. **Evaluate.** Pretend you are on a panel to give an award to Jackie LaFauci and to John Chiesa. List five reasons, in order of importance, why each one should get the award. Use the following outline format.

I. Why Jackie LaFauci deserves the award

A. _____

B. _____

C. _____

D. _____

E. _____

II. Why John Chiesa deserves the award

A. _____

B. _____

C. _____

D. _____

E. _____

DIVERSITY

Applying the Theme and Selections to the Real World

Use a variety of newspapers, magazines, and other reference materials to complete your choice of the following projects or those assigned to you. Also consider using CD-ROM encyclopedias and other on-line databases as well as television programs and videos to get information for your projects.

Interdisciplinary Project 1

Create five interview questions regarding diversity by using information from Selection C. Then interview at least two different owners of businesses in your city or town and chart your answers.

Interdisciplinary Project 2

Watch television and read the newspapers and magazines. Create a chart of ten examples of diversity.

Interdisciplinary Project 3

Research one of your favorite sports teams. Create a collage showing and explaining the differences in race, culture, positions, playing strengths, etc.

Interdisciplinary Project 4

Research the Affirmative Action Laws and the Equal Employment Opportunity Laws. Write a report telling as much as possible about these laws, including some of the actual language in each.

Interdisciplinary Project 5

Write and illustrate a book about your own company. Give it a name and products, and include information about jobs, benefits, worker differences, benefits, diversity, etc.

UNIT 8

The Theme of
HEROISM

HEROISM is action that shows courage while also benefiting others in some way.

PREREADING ACTIVITY

1. Think about acts of heroism.

    a. A firefighter rescues a child from a burning building or a soldier carries a wounded friend to safety during battle.

    b. A group of college students open a shelter for the homeless.

    c. A parent works two jobs to pay for the college education of his or her children.

2. Think about how that action helped others.

    a. A life is saved.

    b. Basic necessities are provided for people who are most needy.

    c. Children receive a good education and are able to get better jobs.

3. Now give two examples of your own of heroic actions and tell how they helped others and how respect is shown.

A first example is done for you.

Example 1. A doctor performs life-saving surgery on a child and receives a distinguished service award from the child's hometown.

Example 2. _____

_____

Example 3. _____

_____

SELECTION A

In Minnesota, which calls itself the "Land of 10,000 Lakes," spring causes the winter ice to melt rapidly. Each year, red signs posted along the banks of lakes and ponds warn of danger. Yet tragedies and near-tragedies occur as the melting ice thins. Most of these thin-ice accidents involve children. They play hockey, take shortcuts home, and challenge the fragile ice in other ways. Here is the story of one such accident.

One warm evening in late March, Ernie Couture was driving home from work. He was sixty-six years old and had been driving that same route for forty years. As he maneuvered the bend at Billings Pond, he saw a dripping-wet golden retriever. The dog was barking frantically and running along the bank. Quickly, Couture pulled over and stopped. He heard faint cries and hurried across the road. He could see two children struggling in the deadly thirty-eight-degree water.

Ernie recalled TV programs he had seen about such emergencies. He pulled off his jacket and outer shirt and carried them with him. He edged onto the ice flat on his stomach. About a hundred feet away in the icy water, two ten-year-old boys cried for help. He could see that they were losing strength.

Ernie inched across the shifting ice. Every move, he knew, was risky. If the ice broke beneath his weight, he would be the third victim of this accident. The final ten feet seemed like ten miles. Near the hole where the boys bobbed in the water, the ice was very thin.

"Hang in there!" Ernie yelled. He threw one end of his jacket to the boy with the weaker voice.

Ernie felt a tug and gave one strong pull. Almost immediately, he had a steel grip on the boy's arm. Carefully, Ernie pulled the boy from the water. He lifted the boy over his back and onto the ice behind him.

By this time a rescue team had arrived. Two paramedics tied long ropes firmly onshore. They approached Ernie and the rescued boy, but the ice was too thin to come nearer. One paramedic tossed a rope toward them. Ernie put a double-hitch around the rescued boy's waist, and the paramedics dragged the boy to safety.

The paramedics threw Ernie a life vest tied to a second long rope. Ernie wrapped himself in the vest and grabbed the rope. Then he dived into the frigid water just as the second boy disappeared. Ernie groped frantically underwater. He found the boy's limp hand and pulled him to the surface. Ernie clung to the child as the paramedics pulled on their lifeline, tugging them both to shore.

Onshore, the heroic paramedics performed CPR (cardiopulmonary resuscitation) on the second boy. A crowd cheered them on. Ernie and the first ten-year-old sat wrapped in blankets. Finally, the second boy choked, sputtered, and began to breathe on his own. The crowd erupted in applause, and the golden retriever barked with joy.

Ernie Couture is a low-key, unassuming man. He did what many people contemplate but rarely experience. Couture risked his own life to rescue two strangers. His quick thinking and daring actions put him in the nation's spotlight.

PRACTICE THE SKILLS

A. Vocabulary Skills

1. Read the following sentences carefully. **As he maneuvered the bend at Billings Pond, he saw a dripping-wet golden retriever. The dog was barking frantically and running along the bank.** Which pair of words best replace **maneuvered** and **frantically** as used in the sentences? (*a*) hit and quietly (*b*) drove and excitedly (*c*) found and loudly (*d*) observed and happily.

2. Use the word **paramedic** in a sentence of your own. _____

3. The world **contemplate** as used in the selection means   (*a*) forget about   (*b*) always enjoy   (*c*) rarely attack   (*d*) think about.

B. Comprehension Skills

1. Copy the sentence that answers the question, **Why didn't the two paramedics help Ernie pull the second boy from the water?**

_____

2. Two important items in the rescue were   (*a*) clothing and ropes   (*b*) ladders and boats   (*c*) life preservers and dogsleds   (*d*) ropes and ice cutters.

3. Which of the following events happened after the first boy was rescued?   (*a*) Ernie threw a life vest to the second boy.   (*b*) The ice gave way under Ernie.   (*c*) Ernie dived into the water.   (*d*) The dog began to bark.

4. The major topic for the minor topics **playing hockey** and **taking shortcuts home** is   (*a*) reasons for cutting school   (*b*) reasons for being on the ice   (*c*) reasons for posting signs   (*d*) things Ernie's children did.

5. Which of the following is the best main idea for the entire selection?
(*a*) Minnesota makes new safety laws for thin ice.
(*b*) Two boys have an accident.
(*c*) Man prevents two drownings in thin-ice accident.
(*d*) Rescue workers perform CPR.

6. The primary cause of drowning from falling through ice is   (*a*) cold weather   (*b*) cold water   (*c*) lack of lifeguards   (*d*) lack of warning signs.

7. Rewrite the following fact into an opinion. **Minnesota is called the "Land of 10,000 Lakes."**

_____

8. You would guess that Ernie's physical condition for a man his age was   (*a*) excellent   (*b*) good   (*c*) fair   (*d*) poor.

Explain your answer. _____

9. You would guess that Ernie's biggest problem in successfully saving the boys was   (*a*) the ice was so thin   (*b*) darkness was setting in   (*c*) the water was getting colder   (*d*) the rescue team had no equipment.

10. Give two reasons why the author thinks that Ernie is a hero. _____

_____

C. Study Skills

1. Complete the following outline with information from the selection.

   I. Five important events in the rescue
   A. Ernie crawled across the ice on his stomach

   B. _____

   C. _____

   D. _____

   E. _____

2. Summarize the contributions of the rescue team in two sentences.

_____

_____

_____

D. Writing Skills

1. Write a one-sentence message or warning that you think should be

posted along bodies of water in the winter. _____

_____

2. Pretend that you are one of the boys in the selection. Write at least four sentences to Ernie thanking him for his heroic deed.

_____

_____

_____

_____

 SELECTION B

Come visit the Genesis ward. It is on the third floor of a big-city hospital in a southwestern state. All of the patients in this ward are children. They are American Indian, African American, white, and Latino. Some are poor and some are wealthy. They suffer the ravages of diseases that cannot be cured, and they are going to die soon. The small patients and their families endure a soon-to-end battle with brain cancer, leukemia, serious heart defects, and other maladies.

Through their daily test of endurance and drug therapy, the children are comforted by nurse Amy Booth, among others. She gives her patients and their visitors wide smiles and comforting messages of cheer and support. Amy works eight hours a day—often more like nine or ten, depending on the needs of her patients.

Some people say that the most important quality of a good doctor or nurse is a bedside manner (how the person treats a patient). Compassion is important, too. Compassion is a deep sympathy and a desire to help people who are suffering. On the Genesis ward, in the face of death, the nurses and doctors show a great deal of compassion. When death is imminent, their acts of heroism are warm smiles, hugs, and just simply being there.

Doctors and nurses receive no formal training on how to smile or hug a patient. They receive no extra pay for working extra hours. Their follow-up calls to patients' families are rewarded only with sincere thank-yous. No newspaper headlines feature their deeds. But they are deeds of heroism, and they are performed every minute of every hour of every day in the Genesis ward by people like Amy Booth.

There are many such quiet heroes, and you can find them everywhere. They are people who get up in the morning and bring a smile, some cheer, and caring service to those in need. We are lucky to have them.

PRACTICE THE SKILLS

A. Vocabulary Skills

1. In the phrase **they suffer the ravages of diseases,** the word **ravages** means (a) good effects (b) bad effects (c) neutral effects (d) curing effects.

2. **Endurance** refers to a person's ability to (a) solve problems (b) ask questions (c) keep going (d) care about other people.

3. **Imminent** means (a) distant (b) enjoyable (c) painful (d) close.

B. Comprehension Skills

1. Copy the two sentences that tell **where this selection takes place.**

_____

_____

2. According to the selection, which two groups of people does Amy Booth deal with the most? (a) doctors and lawyers (b) doctors and the media (c) patients and relatives of patients (d) hospital administrators and lawyers

189

3. What happens after most of the patients enter the Genesis ward? (*a*) They recuperate. (*b*) They die. (*c*) They have operations. (*d*) They become nurses.

4. Give two of the three minor topics from the selection for the major topic **maladies.**

_____

_____

5. Write your own main idea sentence for the selection.

_____

_____

6. According to the selection, what is the cause of patients being placed in the Genesis ward? (*a*) accidents (*b*) diseases (*c*) drug abuse (*d*) all of these

7. Is the final sentence of the selection a fact or an opinion? _____

Explain your answer. _____

_____

8. Why does the author include the sentence **Some are poor and some are wealthy**? _____

_____

9. You would reason that Amy Booth is a good nurse because she is (*a*) dedicated (*b*) well educated (*c*) well-known (*d*) young.

10. The author wrote this selection to show that being a hero is often a simple matter of (*a*) being recognized in the newspaper (*b*) working in a hospital (*c*) working longer hours (*d*) giving comfort to others.

C. Study Skills

1. Complete the following outline with information from the selection.

    I. Five personal and professional qualities of Amy Booth
      A. Willing to work extra hours

      B. _____

      C. _____

      D. _____

      E. _____

2. Complete the following summary sentence. **Amy Booth is a hero**

because _____

_____

D. Writing Skills

1. Copy the one sentence from the selection that you think tells best why Amy Booth is respected. Then explain your choice in one sentence.

_____

_____

_____

2. Write at least four sentences describing someone you know who is a "quiet hero."

_____

_____

_____

_____

SELECTION C

At 8 P.M. on December 11, 1995, a boiler exploded in Malden Mills factory in Lawrence, Massachusetts. Thirty people were injured in the explosion, thirteen of them critically. Some workers escaped after the explosion. Others lay injured inside the burning factory until firefighters rescued them.

Spread by forty-mile-per-hour winds, the fire raged all night. Propane tanks inside the factory exploded. Walls and floors collapsed. Almost three-hundred firefighters from thirty-five nearby communities battled the blaze. By morning, three of the factory's nine buildings had burned to the ground.

Aaron Feuerstein (FUR-steen) owns Malden Mills. His grandfather founded the company in 1906, and his father owned the company before him. Malden Mills produces fabrics. Its lightweight Polartec and Polarfleece fabrics are used in winter jackets. It also produces fabrics for furniture.

Before the fire, more than twenty-four hundred workers, many of them immigrants, toiled forty to fifty hours a week. Many of the workers are second- and third-generation employees of the Feuerstein family. (Their grandparents and parents worked in the factory, too.)

After the fire, the workers were frightened. Would the plant reopen? Feuerstein could collect money from his insurance company and simply close the business. Would they lose their jobs? How would they manage without their paychecks?

Aaron Feuerstein called a meeting of all the workers. He promised that the factory would be rebuilt. He guaranteed them full pay for three months and health insurance for nine months while the factory was being built. He gave an extra Christmas bonus to each worker.

Aaron Feuerstein's employees consider him a hero. He has also been recognized as a hero by the president of the United States. At a recent luncheon in his honor, he was given an award as the Chief Executive Officer (CEO) of the Year. Other testimonials have been given to honor him.

HEROISM

Feuertein says that his employees are his most valuable asset. The decision to keep paying his workers was "the right thing to do." He made this decision easily, he said, based on the religious and cultural legacy of his family. Feuerstein treats his workers with respect, and they respect him for it.

PRACTICE THE SKILLS

A. Vocabulary Skills

1. What is the best context clue for **toiled** in this sentence? **Before the fire, more than two thousand four hundred workers, many of them immigrants, toiled forty to fifty hours a week.**
   (*a*) before the fire   (*b*) more than two thousand four hundred
   (*c*) immigrants   (*d*) forty to fifty hours a week

2. A **testimonial** is an event where   (*a*) profits are announced
   (*b*) bonus checks are given   (*c*) someone is honored
   (*d*) stockholders make decisions.

3. Feuerstein considers his works his most valuable **asset.** What is an **asset**?   (*a*) something of value that you own   (*b*) someone you respect   (*c*) a worker   (*d*) something you owe to someone else

B. Comprehension Skills

1. Facts and information about the effect of the fire on the workers is located in which part of the selection?   (*a*) beginning   (*b*) middle   (*c*) end

   Copy one fact to prove your answer. _____

   _____

2. Before which holiday did the fire occur?   (*a*) Labor Day
   (*b*) Thanksgiving   (*c*) Christmas   (*d*) July Fourth

3. Which event happened first after the fire?   (*a*) Feuerstein was given the CEO of the Year award.   (*b*) The factory was rebuilt.
(*c*) Feuerstein sold the business.   (*d*) Feuerstein provided financial support to his workers.

4. A major topic for the minor topics **pay for three months, health insurance for nine months, extra Christmas bonus** is
(*a*) employee benefits at Malden Mills after the fire   (*b*) Malden Mills workers' demands before the fire   (*c*) employee benefits at all American factories   (*d*) firefighters' demands after the fire.

5. The best main idea sentence is
   (*a*) Aaron Feuerstein is a third-generation owner of the Malden Mills Company.
   (*b*) Aaron Feuerstein is recognized by universities for his leadership skills.
   (*c*) Aaron Feuerstein is considered a hero by his employees.
   (*d*) Aaron Feuerstein is successful.

6. According to the selection, how would you compare Aaron Feuerstein to other owners of a company?   (*a*) about the same   (*b*) somewhat different   (*c*) very different

Explain your answer. _____

_____

7. Add information of your own to the following fact, rewriting it into an opinion. **Treating workers with respect is a corporate**

tradition. _____

_____

_____

8. All of the following are good reasons why the company has lasted so long EXCEPT   (*a*) the way it treats its workers   (*b*) its location
(*c*) the variety and quality of products   (*d*) recognition awards Feuerstein has won.

9. A major problem that Aaron Feuerstein faced after the fire was (*a*) getting support from the president   (*b*) finding new workers (*c*) making decisions   (*d*) reopening quickly.

10. Why does the author show a strong bias in support of Aaron Feuerstein?

_____

How does the author show a strong bias in support of Aaron Feuerstein?

_____

C. Study Skills

1. Complete the following outline with information from the selection.

I. Some facts about Malden Mills

A. _____

B. _____

C. _____

D. A fire destroyed almost all the buildings

II. Some reasons why Aaron Feuerstein is recognized as a hero

A. _____

B. _____

C. _____

D. _____

2. Summarize Feuerstein's thoughts in the last paragraph in one

sentence of your own. _____

_____

D. Writing Skills

1. Write the headline and the first sentence of the story about the Malden Mills fire for a newspaper article. _____

_____

2. Write at least four sentences telling what you learned about how to become a good owner of a company by completing the following. **This is what it takes to be a good owner of a company. First, you need to** _____

_____

Second, you need to _____

Next, you need to _____

Finally, you need to _____

Unit Activities

Reread each selection carefully and then complete the following activities independently or in cooperative groups.

Connecting the Theme and Selections

1. Know. Recall the hero in each selection and the conduct, actions, or deeds of heroism performed. Use the following format for your answers.

In Selection A, the hero is _____ and the act of heroism is

_____

In Selection B, the hero is _____ and the act of heroism is

_____

In Selection C, the hero is _____ and the act of heroism is

_____

2. Comprehend. List the three selections in the order of courage shown by the main character through the deed of heroism. Then give a reason for your first choice.

1. Selection ___ because _____

2. Selection _____

3. Selection _____

3. Apply. Illustrate one of the scenes of heroism in one of the selections with a drawing of your own or with a similar picture from a newspaper or magazine.

4. Analyze. Summarize in one sentence for each selection the motivation of the main character for performing the act of heroism.

5. Synthesize. Compose a song or ballad about one of the heroes in one of the selections.

6. Evaluate. Select the hero in the three selections who will have had the most impact on the most people ten years from now. Give several reasons for your answer in paragraph form.

Applying the Theme and Selections to the Real World

Use a variety of newspapers, magazines, and other reference materials to complete your choice of the following projects or those assigned to you. Also consider using CD-ROM encyclopedias and other on-line databases as well as television programs and videos to get information for your projects.

Interdisciplinary Project 1

Create a collage of five acts of courage and heroism. Include one from an accident, one from medicine, one from business, one from sports, and one from your choice of topic.

Interdisciplinary Project 2

Write a report about two people you know and the deeds of heroism each has performed. Write one paragraph for each hero.

Interdisciplinary Project 3

Research two heroes in American history and summarize the acts of courage and heroism of each in paragraph form. Include pictures or drawings of each hero.

Interdisciplinary Project 4

Write a short story or poem about an imaginary hero and the theme of heroism.

Interdisciplinary Project 5

Write a newspaper editorial giving the reasons for having an annual "Hero Day" or "Courage Day." Give reasons for the holiday and examples of types of heroes we should recognize. Send your final draft to your local newspaper.

UNIT 9

The Theme of
HYPE

HYPE is exaggerated publicity or advertisement for an event or a product in order to increase interest and/or profit.

PREREADING ACTIVITY

1. Think about people, events, or things that are made to be bigger or better than they really are.

   a. A famous Hollywood movie star
   b. A championship football game
   c. A pair of sneakers

2. Think about ways this person, event, or thing is made out to be bigger or better than real life.

   a. Previews in a theater or on a billboard for a new movie
   b. Promotion on television or before other sporting events
   c. Worn by famous athletes in magazine or newspaper advertisements

3. Think about the reasons for the hype associated with the examples. Now give two examples of your own of hype. Include the way that hype is brought about and the reason for the hype.

A first example is provided for you.

Example 1. In the middle of winter, an airline shows sunny and warm islands on television commercials to get people to take a vacation so the airline can make money.

Example 2. _____

_____

Example 3. _____

_____

SELECTION A

In the colder parts of America, you can count on March weather to bring a series of freezes and thaws. Such weather causes "frost heaves" that crack road surfaces and break them up. The result is those awful potholes that seem to come from nowhere overnight. On many a late-winter street or road, a pothole obstacle course challenges the best of drivers.

Would you believe that a pothole could cause hype? (Hype is elaborate, exaggerated promotion or advertising.) Believe it or not, there are annual pothole contests in some parts of the United States. In Rochester, New Hampshire ("the Lilac City"), for example, there is a yearly pothole contest. The city newspaper and area businesses sponsor the event.

The entry process is simple. Just send in a postcard with your favorite pothole or street of potholes along with a nickname for it. Four winners are chosen annually. Recent winners have included Bronco Boulevard, Muffler Mangler, Dire on Tires, and Clark Road Crater.

First prize is a free four-wheel alignment and a three-foot trophy from an area tire company. The second prize is a front-wheel alignment and a one-foot trophy from a different tire company. The third-prize winner gets a flat tire mounted on an old rusted rim. The winner's name is inscribed on the rim. Fourth prize is a humorous T-shirt emblazoned with the message, "Surf's up—come ride the heaves."

The closing date for pothole contest entries is always March 19. Winners are announced in the next edition of Rochester's weekly newspaper.

PRACTICE THE SKILLS

A. Vocabulary Skills

1. The word **sponsor** as used in the phrase **businesses sponsor the event** means   (a) do not want   (b) sell tickets to   (c) support   (d) write about.

2. Copy the following sentence and replace the word **annually** with a new word or phrase of your own. **Four winners are chosen annually.** _____

_____

3. What other word used in the fourth paragraph means about the same as the word **inscribed**? (*a*) mounted (*b*) humorous (*c*) emblazoned (*d*) announced

_____

Explain your answer using context clues such as **name, T-shirt, message.** _____

_____

_____

B. Comprehension Skills

1. What are the names of the winning potholes? The information needed to answer this question is located in which paragraph? (*a*) first (*b*) second (*c*) third (*d*) fourth

2. According to the selection, what causes potholes? (*a*) car accidents (*b*) alternating freezes and thaws (*c*) heavy traffic (*d*) earthquakes and tornadoes

3. Which of the following occurs BEFORE March 19? (*a*) Contest winners are chosen. (*b*) Contest winners are announced in the newspaper. (*c*) Prizes are awarded to contest winners. (*d*) Businesses get involved in the contest.

4. The best major topic for the minor topics **Bronco Boulevard, Muffler Mangler, Dire on Tires,** and **Clark Road Crater** is (*a*) names of businesses (*b*) names of prizes (*c*) names of streets and potholes (*d*) names of newspapers.

5. Write a title for this selection. _____

_____

6. The effect of **freeze, thaw, freeze, thaw** is   (a) longer nights
(b) frost heaves   (c) flu outbreak   (d) easier driving.

7. Is the first sentence of the selection a fact or an opinion? Explain your answer.

_____

_____

How about the last sentence of the selection?   _____

_____

_____

8. You would think that potholes cause the most damage to which part of the car?   (a) mufflers   (b) windows   (c) steering wheels (d) tires

9. Who gains the most from the pothole contest?   (a) the residents of the winning streets   (b) the weekly newspaper   (c) construction companies   (d) the companies that make the trophies

Explain your answer.   _____

_____

_____

10. The author's purpose in writing this selection was to give you   (a) a worthwhile contest to enter   (b) an example of hype   (c) good driving instructions   (d) a lesson about weather.

C. Study Skills

1. Complete the following outline with information from the selection.

I. _____

   A. First prize
     1. Four-wheel alignment
     2. Three-foot trophy

B. _____

    1. _____

    2. _____

C. _____

    1. _____

D. _____

    1. _____

2. Summarize how potholes form by completing the following sentence with your own information. **Potholes form when** _____

_____

D. Writing Skills

1. Write a one-sentence radio commercial or slogan that hypes the contest and gets someone to enter before the deadline.

_____

_____

2. Write at least four sentences for a newspaper article that describes the winning entries in this year's contest. Make up the names of the winning potholes or streets and make up different prizes.

_____

_____

_____

_____

HYPE

SELECTION B

Can you name the three major American sporting events that receive the most hype? Think awhile and see if you can name the Big Three.

Ready for the answers?

- Super Sunday and the Super Bowl in late January
- The World Series (especially a Game 7) in October
- The Final Four of college basketball and the championship game two days later. (This whole tournament is nicknamed March Madness.)

Americans' love for sports is unmatched in any other country. One exception might be the World Cup for soccer every four years. European countries, such as Spain and Germany, and South American countries, such as Brazil and Colombia, go wild over World Cup soccer.

But what price do we Americans pay for our love of sports? We wade through weeks of seemingly endless elimination games and playoffs. Newspapers, magazines, and airwaves are saturated with sports promotions and advertising. All this hype builds up to that big kickoff, first pitch, or championship tipoff.

The hype of championship sports includes interviews with people connected to larger-than-life athletes. In these interviews, boyhood friends, high school coaches, and even grandmothers recall what a famous athlete was like as a young person. Around each promotion, advertisement, and interview are products carefully marketed to different audiences.

Championship day is a bonanza for people selling sports-related items. Tickets sell for several thousand dollars each. Sportswear and souvenirs are hawked onsite and around the country. During the event, a thirty-second television commercial costs more than $1 million. On TV, creative, colorful ads try to persuade viewers to buy cereal, cars, sneakers, soft drinks, and dozens of other products. As always, each ad suggests that buying the product will improve your life.

HYPE

When the championship ends, the glitz and glamour of the super event hype dry up faster than a desert raindrop. But, of course, the cycle continues. A never-ending menu of TV sports provides a year-round feast for viewers. And though it may not be as intense as for the Big Three championship events, sports hype is with us all year long.

PRACTICE THE SKILLS

A. Vocabulary Skills

1. The word **saturated** means   (a) empty   (b) filled   (c) wet   (d) none of these.

2. In the sentence **Championship day is a bonanza for people selling sports-related items,** the best context clue to understand the meaning of **bonanza** is   (a) Championship   (b) day   (c) people selling   (d) none of these.

   Explain your answer. _____

   _____

3. Rewrite the sentence in which the word **hawked** is used. Replace **hawked** with a new word of your own. _____

   _____

B. Comprehension Skills

1. Copy the sentence that contains the information to answer the question, **How long is a TV commercial in a championship game, and how much does it cost**?

   _____

   _____

HYPE

2. Three sports mentioned in the selection are   (*a*) golf, football, baseball   (*b*) football, baseball, hockey   (*c*) car racing, basketball, soccer   (*d*) football, baseball, basketball.

3. The last event in March Madness is   (*a*) the Final Four   (*b*) the championship game   (*c*) Game 7 of the World Series   (*d*) the World Cup.

4. Name the four minor topics in the selection for the major topic

kinds of products advertised. _____

5. Choose the best main idea for the selection.
  (*a*) The hype in sports such as football is the most enjoyable part of life.
  (*b*) The hype of a championship sports event is seen most in America.
  (*c*) The hype of sports events is part of American life.
  (*d*) The hype of all sports is needed to maintain a good life.

6. All three American sporting events in the selection can be compared best in the area of   (*a*) number of fans   (*b*) number of investors   (*c*) number of playoff games   (*d*) amount of hype and advertising.

7. Is the following sentence a fact or an opinion? **Newspapers, magazines, and airwaves are saturated with sports promotions and advertising.** Explain.

_____

_____

8. You would conclude that the words **kickoff, pitch, tipoff** as used in the selection refer most to   (*a*) specific promotions   (*b*) specific sports   (*c*) specific athletes   (*d*) specific months.

9. The problem that seems to be presented in the selection is that major sports events   (*a*) cost too much to attend   (*b*) are scheduled too close to one another   (*c*) promote too much junk food   (*d*) often don't live up to the pregame hype.

10. Does the author's overall attitude seem to be one of like or dislike of sports?

Explain your answer. _____

_____

_____

C. Study Skills

1. Complete the following outline with information from the selection.

   I. Sporting events described in the selection
     A. Super Bowl—late January

     B. _____

     C. _____

  II. Types of hype in sports events

     A. _____

     B. _____

     C. _____
     D. Sportswear and souvenirs

 III. _____
     A. Cereal

     B. _____

     C. _____

     D. _____

2. Summarize the information given in the last paragraph by completing the following sentence. **The last paragraph is about** _____

_____

_____

D. Writing Skills

1. Choose a product or a food that you like. Write a one-sentence advertisement that promotes that product or food in one of the Big Three events in the selection.

2. Write a four- to seven-sentence editorial for one of the major sports magazines. Suggest a major sporting event that you think should be added to the Big Three list. State your opinion and give reasons to support it. Begin your editorial with the following.

Number four on the list of the Big Four sporting events is

_____

_____

_____

_____

SELECTION C

The following advertisement for a new automobile called the Starflight is hype for the senses. See how it tries to persuade you to test-drive and buy a Starflight.

You worked for it—you earned it! Now it's time to enjoy the luxury and elegance of the new Starflight. Easing into your seat in this flight in shining armor is like easing into first class on a plane to Hawaii. It's the flight of your lifetime. Leave your problems behind as the road becomes your route to paradise.

If you have an appetite for total quality, you'll find Starflight both *nutritious* and *delicious*. Event its luxury aroma is inviting.

Elegance in engineering provides total comfort and safety to driver and passengers with Starflight's unique design features.

HYPE

- The 24-valve fuel-injected V-6 allows free-breathing and precise fuel distribution.
- The four-speed automatic transmission with special standard overdrive adjusts to your driving habits and road conditions.
- Each passenger has total control over seat adjustment. Rear passengers can elevate their seats slightly above the front for better communication.
- Every Starflight has two impact bumpers in the front and steel high-impact beams in each door.

Yes, you can have the ride of your lifetime, and it can last as long as you like. When you step inside a Starflight, time is endless. The sky's the limit for reaching total control, comfort, and reward in your driving experience!

Come fly with Starflight!

PRACTICE THE SKILLS

A. Vocabulary Skills

1. The words **luxury** and **elegance** as used in the phrase **enjoy the the luxury and elegance of the new Starflight** could be replaced with the words (*a*) speed and handling (*b*) price and maintenance (*c*) comfort and richness (*d*) size and advertising.

2. The word **aroma** refers to which sense? (*a*) sight (*b*) sound (*c*) touch (*d*) smell

3. In the phrase **precise fuel distribution,** the word **precise** means (*a*) costly (*b*) exact (*c*) polluting (*d*) extensive.

B. Comprehension Skills

1. How many design features of the Starflight are described in the selection? (*a*) two (*b*) three–five (*c*) seven–ten (*d*) more than ten

211

HYPE

2. Which group of people receive the most hype for the Starflight in the selection? (*a*) salespeople and mechanics (*b*) people who write ads and travel agents (*c*) passengers and drivers (*d*) television and radio announcers

3. All of the hype in the advertisement takes place mostly (*a*) before a purchase (*b*) after a purchase (*c*) during trade-in for a new car (*d*) during maintenance checkups.

4. The best major topic for the minor topics **24-valve, fuel-injected, V-6** is (*a*) design features for control (*b*) design features for performance (*c*) design features for safety (*d*) design features for comfort.

5. Write a one-sentence main idea for the entire selection. Include the words **hype, Starflight, and purchase** in your sentence. _____

_____

6. The selection compares the Starflight driving experience to all of the following EXCEPT a (*a*) vacation site (*b*) meal (*c*) plane ride (*d*) sports event.

7. Is the selection mostly fact or opinion? Explain your answer by discussing whether hype is mostly fact or opinion. _____

_____

_____

8. Explain why you think the car is named Starflight. _____

_____

_____

9. You would reason that the hype for the Starflight appeals mostly to a driver's need to (*a*) buy affordable transportation (*b*) satisfy the desire for luxury and elegance (*c*) provide safety for family members (*d*) travel to new vacation sites.

Explain your answer. _____

_____

212

10. The author seems to show the hype for automobiles as
(*a*) excessive and appealing   (*b*) costly and ineffective   (*c*) decreasing
and unaccepted   (*d*) increasing and more visual.

C. Study Skills

1. Complete the following outline with information from the selection.

   I. Statements of hype related to flying
     A. Flight in shining armor

     B. _____

     C. _____

  II. Statements of hype related to design
     A. Provides the driver and passenger with total comfort and
       safety

     B. _____

     C. _____

     D. _____
     E. Impact beams in the doors

2. Write one well-written sentence that summarizes why you should or
should not buy a Starflight. _____

_____

D. Writing Skills

1. Copy the sentence that you think contains the most important
reason or appeal to the buyer and rewrite it into your own words.

_____

_____

HYPE

2. You have made a final decision about a Starflight. Write at least four sentences with your decision to buy or not to buy and give at least three reasons for your decision.

I have decided _____

_____

_____

_____

_____

Unit Activities

Reread each selection carefully and then complete the following activities independently or in cooperative groups.

Connecting the Theme and Selections

1. Know. List the general event or thing that is hyped in each selection. Use the following format.

Potholes were hyped in Selection A.

_____ in Selection B.

_____ in Selection C.

2. Comprehend. Explain which selection has the most hype for the most people. Give at least three reasons for your choice.

3. Apply. Apply one advertising slogan of your own for each selection that could be used to hype the event or product.

Selection A. _____

Selection B. _____

Selection C. _____

214

4. Analyze. Chart the selections in order of advertising expenses.

Least cost—Selection ———
Middle cost—Selection ———
Most cost—Selection ———

5. Synthesize. Choose one of the Big Three sports events in Selection B. Create your own thirty-second television commercial with that sport in mind that hypes the Starflight from Selection C. For example, the opening scene shows two beautiful people stepping into a sparkling Starflight. How would you add information related to the sports event for use in a commercial?

6. Evaluate. Grade the hype presented in Selections A and C on a scale of A to F with A being excellent and F a failure. Give several reasons for the grade that you give.

Applying the Theme and Selections to the Real World

Use a variety of newspapers, magazines, and other reference materials to complete your choice of the following projects or those assigned to you. Also consider using CD-ROM encyclopedias and other on-line databases as well as television programs and videos to get information for your projects.

Interdisciplinary Project 1

Assess the importance of hype in advertising and write a three-paragraph editorial either supporting hype or opposing hype. Explain what hype is in the first paragraph. Explain examples of hype in the second paragraph. Give very specific reasons to support your position in the third paragraph. Send a copy to your local newspaper.

Interdisciplinary Project 2

Choose an existing product and give examples of hype associated with that product. Then invent an original product of your own. Give it a name and create several examples of hype for it, including appropriate visual graphics.

Interdisciplinary Project 3

Choose five different products on the market and five different events scheduled for upcoming weeks or months. Create a collage of hype showing the five products and the five events.

Interdisciplinary Project 4

Review the television and movie guide in a magazine or newspaper. Choose five television programs and five movies. Copy the most appealing phrases of hype for each program or movie.

Interdisciplinary Project 5

Watch television and take notes about five different commercials. Create a chart of the following information for each commercial.

1. The product or event
2. The audience that the product or event appeals to
3. The hype given to persuade you to purchase the product or see the event
4. The slogan or outstanding statement of hype
5. A statement of opinion about the effect of the hype (will you purchase the product or see the event?)

UNIT 10

The Theme of
INVENTION

Definition

INVENTION is a product or a process that enables us to do something new, or makes it easier to do something old.

PREREADING ACTIVITY

1. Observe all the things around you that had to come about through invention.

    a. Automobiles and airplanes; rockets and submarines
    b. Refrigerators and washing machines
    c. Cardiopulmonary resuscitation (CPR) and wheelchairs

2. Think about how each one of these has improved something else.

    a. Daily transportation; military security for the country
    b. Preserving food and keeping clothing clean
    c. Sustaining life after heart failure and aids for handicapped people

3. Now give two examples of your own of inventions and how each improved something else.

> ### *The first example is done for you.*

Example 1. The study of polio caused the development of a vaccine in the 1950s that prevented a serious disease.

Example 2. _____

_____

Example 3. _____

_____

SELECTION A

Imagine what the world would be like without telephones, television, computers, and motion pictures. These things didn't always exist. Someone—sometimes a group of people—invented them.

Inventions play an important role in human history. Inventions and innovations (new ways of doing things) usually are created to fill business, military, social, or medical needs.

How many really important inventions can you name? The list is very long and will continue to grow. First, let's look at three very old inventions that have impacted human life in important ways.

At the top of the list is the wheel. No one knows for sure who thought of the first wheel, but historians think the wheel was invented around 3000 B.C. That's five thousand years ago. The wheel made it possible to transport people and farm goods in carts pulled by oxen or horses.

Some two thousand years ago, the ancient Romans invented the aqueduct. An aqueduct is a channel or trough that allows water to move from one point or elevation to another. This invention was a crude form of plumbing. It provided fresh water for people as well as water for irrigating farmland.

Around 1426, a German printer named Johann Gutenberg printed the first book in Europe. He used movable type and a printing press. (Earlier forms of printing had existed in Korea and in Japan.) Before Gutenberg, monks and scribes wrote manuscripts by hand—one at a time. Because such manuscripts were so expensive, the common people never saw them. After Gutenberg, printed books became widely and cheaply available. People learned to read. Literacy and education became goals for developing societies.

Now let's look at three important inventions from the nineteenth and twentieth centuries.

Gasoline-powered automobiles first hit the road in 1885. German engineers invented a three-wheeled automobile and then a four-wheeled version. The automobile replaced horse-driven carriages, wagons, and carts. With the automobile, people could travel farther, faster, and more cheaply.

In 1892, Rudolf Diesel invented the diesel engine. It provides heavy-duty power and runs on low-cost fuel. Diesel engines power construction equipment, trucks, buses, train locomotives, and jet engines.

The computer is just as revolutionary today as Gutenberg's printing press was in the 1400s. Unlike other machines, computers have memory. The first information-processing computer was built by an American engineer in 1944. Personal computers, the kind you use, began to appear in the 1980s.

These are just six of the thousands of inventions humans have devised. What will be next? What do you imagine might be the next really important invention?

PRACTICE THE SKILLS

A. Vocabulary Skills

1. The word **impacted** as used in the selection could be replaced best with the word   (a) cost   (b) hurt   (c) affected   (d) provided.

2. **Aqueducts** transport   (a) people   (b) water   (c) food   (d) animals.

3. **Literacy** as used in the selection means the same as what other word used in the selection?   (a) education   (b) gasoline (c) mankind   (d) computer

B. Comprehension Skills

1. In what time period was the printing press invented?   (a) 3000 B.C. (b) 1400s   (c) 1800s   (d) 1900s

2. Which of the following would NOT use diesel power?   (a) irrigation (b) train locomotive   (c) jet airplane   (d) construction equipment

221

3. Which innovation was first introduced after the gasoline automobile?
(*a*) wheels   (*b*) computer   (*c*) diesel engine   (*d*) dams

4. The major topic for the minor topics **economic, military, social, medical** is   (*a*) reasons for inventions   (*b*) famous Greek inventions   (*c*) recent inventions   (*d*) uses of the wheel.

5. The best title for this selection is
(*a*) Greek and Roman Innovations and Inventions
(*b*) A Look at Future Innovations and Inventions
(*c*) Inventions for Improved Farming
(*d*) Inventions Old and New

6. The best comparison of the printing press and the computer is that each is able to put words or language into permanent form for others to read. Now explain in your own words the best contrast of

the printing press and the computer. _____

_____

_____

7. Copy one fact about one invention. Then rewrite it into an opinion.

_____

_____

_____

8. You would think that most inventors seem to have a good background in   (*a*) geography   (*b*) history   (*c*) mechanics   (*d*) literature.

9. You would guess that the most important need for innovations and inventions in early times was in the area of   (*a*) medicine   (*b*) transportation   (*c*) housekeeping   (*d*) education.

Explain your answer. _____

_____

10. The author's purpose in writing this selection is to   (*a*) give information   (*b*) tell a story   (*c*) solve a problem   (*d*) describe a famous person.

C. Study Skills

1. Complete the following outline with information from the selection.

I. Famous inventions before 1800

A. _____

B. _____

C. _____

II. _____

A. The gasoline automobile in 1885

B. _____

C. _____

2. Summarize what you think is the most important innovation or invention described in the selection. Give a reason for your choice.

_____

_____

_____

D. Writing Skills

1. Write one sentence describing what you think is an important invention today that is not described in the selection. Include a reason for your choice.

_____

_____

2. Write at least four sentences explaining what you think are the major qualities of an inventor. In other words, how do you become an inventor? _____

_____

_____

_____

_____

 SELECTION B

     Consider the number of planes that take off every few minutes from every major airport in the United States. Add the planes from military bases. Next, add the small aircraft from local "mom-and-pop" airports. Finally, add the incoming commercial flights from other countries.

     Every day and night the sky is filled with planes. How is all this traffic controlled? And why is flying statistically the safest form of travel?

     After World War II, passenger air travel "took off." The 1950s postwar economy was a boon for the airline industry. Wartime technology shifted to domestic and passenger airplanes. For all of these reasons, the government created the Federal Aviation Administration (FAA) in 1958. This agency regulates air traffic both on the ground and in flight.

     The job of air traffic controller is one of the most technical and vital in America. It is also one of the most stressful. There is no room for error. Like pilots, air traffic controllers undergo rigorous training.

     Radar, telecommunications, and computers are the tools controllers use to coordinate air traffic. Each flight's takeoff, landing, and flight pattern are predetermined. During every flight, controllers and pilots are in constant communication to assure that those patterns are kept. It is this constant communication that makes air travel so safe.

All the inventions in the world can't completely eliminate the possibility of malfunction or human error. That is why there is no letup in air traffic control until a plane is at the gate and the pilot shuts off its engines.

PRACTICE THE SKILLS

A. Vocabulary Skills

1. When something is **predetermined,** it is   (*a*) unplanned   (*b*) not possible   (*c*) planned in advance   (*d*) stubborn.

2. The best word to replace the word **assure** as used in the selection is   (*a*) decide   (*b*) guarantee   (*c*) avoid   (*d*) save.

3. In the sentence containing the word **malfunction,** the best context clue to figure out the meaning of **malfunction** is   (*a*) inventions   (*b*) world   (*c*) possibility   (*d*) error.

B. Comprehension Skills

1. Copy the sentence that contains the information to answer the question, **What does the FAA do?** _____

_____

2. According to the selection, which of the following is the safest form of travel?   (*a*) bicycle   (*b*) automobile   (*c*) train   (*d*) airplane

3. The need for air traffic control of passenger planes began   (*a*) right after World War I   (*b*) soon after World War II   (*c*) during the 1960s   (*d*) during the 1980s and 1990s.

4. Choose a word from the selection that is a major topic for the minor topics **radar, telecommunications, computers.** _____

5. Which of the following phrases is the best main idea of the selection?   (*a*) Federal Aviation Administration   (*b*) air traffic control (*c*) 1950s postwar economy   (*d*) pilots and crew members

6. Which of the following sentences gives the cause for stress associated with the job of air traffic controller?

(*a*) Finally, add the incoming commercial flights from other countries.
(*b*) This agency regulates air traffic both on the ground and in flight.
(*c*) There is no room for error.
(*d*) Each flight's takeoff, landing, and flight pattern are predetermined.

7. Most of the statements in the selection are   (*a*) facts   (*b*) opinions (*c*) an equal number of facts and opinions.

8. You would guess that the air traffic controller's "best friend" to maintain safety is the   (*a*) weather   (*b*) travel agent   (*c*) computer (*d*) overseas flight.

9. What is needed most for safe takeoffs, landings, and flight patterns? (*a*) planning and communication   (*b*) military support   (*c*) modern airports   (*d*) FAA-trained pilots

10. The author probably believes the greatest need associated with air travel is to make it   (*a*) cheaper   (*b*) comfortable   (*c*) convenient (*d*) safer.

C. Study Skills

1. Complete the following outline with information from the selection.

I. Three reasons for the FAA
    A. More air travel after World War II

    B. _____

    C. _____

II. _____

    A. Radar

    B. _____

    C. _____

2. Give two reasons to summarize why the job of air traffic controller is stressful. **The job of air traffic controller is stressful because**

_____

_____

_____

D. Writing Skills

1. Copy one sentence from the selection that you think best explains why the job of air traffic controller or pilot is so important. Then rewrite that sentence in your own words. _____

_____

_____

2. Which job do you think is more stressful, air traffic controller or pilot? Explain your answer in at least four sentences. _____

_____

_____

_____

SELECTION C

As America moves into the twenty-first century, specific issues and problems will require our attention. Our aging population is sure to be at the top of the list. In the twenty-first century, America will have more older people than younger. More people will live into their eighties and nineties than ever before.

One of the major needs of the aging population will be maintaining and expanding medical research. This research is necessary to develop innovative treatments for serious diseases.

One of the most serious is Alzheimer's disease. Currently, about four million people suffer the effects of Alzheimer's. Most are over sixty-five, but the disease can strike people in their forties. Alzheimer's is a disease that destroys brain cells and their functions. Unlike other kinds of cells, brain cells do not regenerate (regrow or replace dead cells). At present, there is neither a treatment nor a cure.

Brain cells are needed to support basic functions. These include memory, coherent speech, and motor control, such as walking and eating. As the disease advances, a person with Alzheimer's loses almost all independence. Victims of this disease need constant physical care. They tend to be depressed and need psychological care also. The entire family suffers.

Research scientists now have an "eye" on early detection of Alzheimer's. Scientists at Harvard Medical School have developed an easy test. It involves a simple eye exam and the drug tropicamide. This drug dilates, or enlarges, the pupil of the eye.

Researchers studied patients in nearby hospitals whose average age was seventy-two. They found that the pupils of healthy patients dilate only 4 percent. In contrast, the pupils of patients with Alzheimer's dilate 13 percent. Several patients who had no symptoms of the disease but who had larger percentages of dilation developed Alzheimer's within a year.

What is important about these results? Ongoing research is aimed at slowing the advancement of the disease. A drug or test that can diagnose the disease early would give doctors, patients, and their families hope. They can hope for better quality of life in the present and a treatment or cure in the near future.

INVENTION

PRACTICE THE SKILLS

A. Vocabulary Skills

1. Copy the context clue that explains the meaning of the word
regenerate. _____

_____

2. The word **coherent** as used in the phrase **coherent speech** means
(*a*) loud   (*b*) educated   (*c*) public   (*d*) understandable.

3. What is the difference between **physical** and **psychological care**?

_____

_____

B. Comprehension Skills

1. What does the drug tropicamide do?   (*a*) treats Alzheimer's disease
(*b*) dilates the pupils   (*c*) assists families   (*d*) cures other diseases

2. Depression requires   (*a*) physical care   (*b*) psychological care
(*c*) motor control   (*d*) independence.

3. As the disease advances or becomes more serious for a victim, which
of the following groups suffers the most?   (*a*) doctors
(*b*) researchers   (*c*) families   (*d*) all Americans

4. Choose three minor topics from the selection that would come under
the major topic **functions of the brain.** _____

_____

5. Complete the following to give a main idea for the entire selection.
Alzheimer's disease _____

_____

6. Which of the following is the most serious effect of Alzheimer's disease? (*a*) loss of independence (*b*) loss of eyesight (*c*) loss of appetite (*d*) loss of family support

7. Copy a fact from the selection about Alzheimer's disease that concerns you the most. Then explain why it concerns you the most.

_____

_____

8. The reason that there is likely to be an increase in the number of Alzheimer's patients is (*a*) there will be more older Americans (*b*) there will be less health insurance (*c*) there will be less tropicamide (*d*) there will be more hospitals.

9. The best medical solutions for the problems of Alzheimer's disease are focused on all of the following EXCEPT (*a*) earlier detection (*b*) a cure (*c*) quality care (*d*) better health insurance.

10. The author is most sympathetic to which group? (*a*) families of Alzheimer victims (*b*) doctors (*c*) scientists (*d*) healthy older Americans

Explain your answer. _____

_____

C. Study Skills

1. Complete the following outline with information from the selection.

    I. Five things I learned about Alzheimer's disease
       A. First, I learned that it is usually a disease of older people

       B. _____

       C. _____

       D. _____

       E. _____

II. Three things I learned about the eyes and Alzheimer's disease
    A. First, I learned that scientists are giving eye exams to people with Alzheimer's

    B. _____

    C. _____

2. Since there is neither a treatment nor a cure for Alzheimer's, summarize in two sentences what should be available for a person with Alzheimer's disease.

_____

_____

_____

_____

D. Writing Skills

1. If you were interviewing a scientist at Harvard Medical School, write two questions that you would like to ask about Alzheimer's disease.

_____

_____

_____

2. Write a personal note of at least four sentences to an Alzheimer's patient at home or in the hospital. _____

_____

_____

_____

_____

Unit Activities

Reread each selection carefully and then complete the following activities independently or in cooperative groups.

Connecting the Theme and Selections

1. **Know.** Identify a major invention in each selection.

   In Selection A, a major invention was _____

   In Selection B, a major invention was _____

   In Selection C, a major invention was _____

2. **Comprehend.** Describe one invention from the three selections that most affects humankind, with three reasons for your choice. Use the following format.

   The invention of _____ in Selection ____ most affects humankind.

   Reason 1. _____

   Reason 2. _____

   Reason 3. _____

3. **Apply.** Imagine that you could interview the inventor of one of the inventions in Selection A. Write three questions that you would ask. Then answer each question. Use the following format.

   Question 1. _____

   Answer. _____

   _____

   _____

INVENTION

Question 2. _____

Answer. _____

_____

_____

Question 3. _____

Answer. _____

_____

_____

4. **Analyze.** Analyze the innovations and inventions in Selection A. Choose one in Selection A that is necessary for the success of the innovation in Selection B and one that is necessary for the success of the innovation in Selection C. Use paragraph form for each answer.

5. **Synthesize.** Fantasize that you are observing the inventor of the wheel some five thousand years ago as he or she is in the final stages of the invention. In one paragraph, describe what you are observing.

6. **Evaluate.** Rate the following five inventions from the selections from 1 to 5, 1 being most important: **Aqueduct, Gasoline Engine, Computer, Air Traffic Control, Tropicamide.** Next to each give a reason for your choice. Use the following format.

1 is _____ because _____

2 is _____ because _____

3 is _____ because _____

4 is _____ because _____

5 is _____ because _____

INVENTION

Applying the Theme and Selections to the Real World

Use a variety of newspapers, magazines, and other reference materials to complete your choice of the following projects or those assigned to you. Also consider using CD-ROM encyclopedias and other on-line databases as well as television programs and videos to get information for your projects.

Interdisciplinary Project 1

Research one invention or innovation for each major sport in America—basketball, baseball, hockey, and football. The innovation might be a rule such as the 3-point shot in basketball or the 2-point conversion in football. Or an invention such as the goalie mask in hockey or the aluminum bat in baseball. Create a collage of your four innovations or inventions and write a descriptive paragraph about each one. Also include information about why it was needed and how it improved the sport.

Interdisciplinary Project 2

Research one American male and one female innovator or inventor. Explain the innovation or invention with pictures in a report.

Interdisciplinary Project 3

Research a disease. Write a report describing the current status of that disease regarding treatment and possible cure.

Interdisciplinary Project 4

Create an innovation or an invention to respond to a need in our society. Tell all about it in a report with pictures or drawings. Include some of the problems you had as an innovator or inventor.

Interdisciplinary Project 5

Create a report of your choices of the most important innovation or invention in history for each of the following categories: agriculture, communication, medicine, military, transportation, and manufacturing. Include the following information: date invented, description, inventor, function of the invention. Also include as many pictures or drawings as possible.

UNIT 11

The Theme of
JUSTICE

Definition

JUSTICE is truth and fairness; it is the reward or punishment deserved for an action.

PREREADING ACTIVITY

1. Think about examples of justice that you have seen or have gone through.

   a. A new student in school who helps other students is elected to a class office, while the current officeholder who is very snobbish and a member of a clique is defeated.
   b. A neighborhood petty thief is caught by the police in the act of stealing a bicycle.
   c. A judge rules that a politician used his position to get construction contracts for family members in the construction business.

2. Think about the reward or punishment for each.

   a. Decision making at the school is open to more students.
   b. Community service has to be performed.
   c. The politician falls in the public opinion polls and resigns from office.

3. Now give two examples of your own of justice, one with a reward and one with a punishment.

> **A first example is done for you.**

Example 1. A mother whose husband was killed some years ago sees her son's high school graduation and acceptance to Harvard University.

Example 2. _____

_____

Example 3. _____

_____

SELECTION A

The Declaration of Independence proclaims that "life, liberty, and the pursuit of happiness" are self-evident rights. To these, the United States Constitution adds "domestic tranquility" and "the blessings of liberty." Civil rights laws passed in the 1960s enforce these basic rights for all citizens. According to these rights, all Americans have the right to live in their homes without being harassed by neighbors.

A judge in a large midwestern city recently ruled on a case that tested these rights. The setting was a racially and culturally mixed neighborhood. For nine years, one family had been harassing their next-door neighbors. They hurled racial epithets. They destroyed property. They threatened bodily harm. Finally, the family that suffered the nine years of torment sued their neighbors. They filed a multimillion-dollar lawsuit.

A judge listened to all of the evidence. What do you think the judge's decision was?

The judge decreed that the harassers must sell their house within 180 days. They must leave the neighborhood. The judge further decreed that he would punish the harassers if they did not abide by his decision. If they did not move, their additional penalty would be to pay a thousand dollars a month to the family they had victimized.

A lawyer who is a member of a local civil rights group commented on the judge's actions. "If you hold bigoted views . . . , you may be the one who will have to move out."

PRACTICE THE SKILLS

A. Vocabulary Skills

1. In the phrase **domestic tranquility, domestic** means **at home** or **in the neighborhood. Tranquility** means   (*a*) violence   (*b*) escape   (*c*) peacefulness   (*d*) wealth.

2. Which of the following situations involves the word **violating**? (*a*) driving faster than the speed limit   (*b*) giving a gift to a friend (*c*) finding a lost wallet   (*d*) working late on a homework assignment

3. Epithets are   (*a*) weapons   (*b*) words   (*c*) books   (*d*) dollars.

B.   Comprehension Skills

1. Which paragraph contains the most information about what the harassers did to their neighbors?   (*a*) first   (*b*) second   (*c*) third (*d*) fourth

2. The major decision of the judge about how to settle the problem involves   (*a*) the police   (*b*) forcing the neighbors to separate (*c*) apologies   (*d*) jail time.

3. The case went to court after how many years?   (*a*) one   (*b*) five (*c*) nine   (*d*) fifteen

4. The major topic for the minor topics **domestic tranquility, pursuit of happiness, civil rights** is _____

5. The best title for this selection is
   (*a*) Bigotry Doesn't Pay
   (*b*) City Property Values Decline
   (*c*) New Neighbors Needed
   (*d*) Judge Praises Neighbors' Actions

6. As a result of the actions of the harassers, the family that was harassed   (*a*) moved from the neighborhood   (*b*) destroyed property of the harassers   (*c*) took a vacation   (*d*) filed a lawsuit.

7. Is the last sentence of the selection a fact or an opinion? _____

Explain your answer. _____

_____

8. Which of the following actions of the harassers did NOT happen? (a) racial epithets   (b) destruction of property   (c) threats to do bodily harm   (d) stolen motor vehicle

9. Why do you think the family that was harassed remained in the neighborhood for nine years of harassment? _____

_____

_____

10. The author's purpose in writing this selection is to give an example of   (a) how a problem can be solved   (b) why fines are important (c) how the court system works   (d) why big-city neighborhoods are good places to live.

C. Study Skills

1. Complete the following outline with information from the selection.

    I. Acts committed by the harassers
      A. Hurled racial epithets

      B. _____

      C. _____

    II. Three decisions in the case

      A. _____

      B. _____

      C. _____

2. Summarize in one or two sentences how one of the rights mentioned in the first paragraph applies to the selection. _____

_____

_____

D. Writing Skills

1. Rewrite the last sentence of the selection into a new sentence of your own. Keep the same meaning but use your own words.

_____

_____

2. Give your opinion about the decisions in the case. Did justice occur for one or both families? Why or why not? Write at least four sentences. _____

_____

_____

_____

_____

_____

 SELECTION B

Mrs. Priscilla Archie makes her way proudly to the podium. Tonight, after forty-four years of teaching, she is retiring. She has taught thousands of elementary school students. She can name every one of her former students and tell an anecdote or special story about each one of them. Many are in the audience tonight.

Tonight, Mrs. Archie is being honored by family, friends, students, and community. They have already thanked her for her tireless efforts. The mayor has given her the key to the city. Her portrait has been unveiled. It will hang in the foyer of the school. She has been glowing with pride at the many comments about her lifetime of service to young people.

Mrs. Archie pauses before she begins to speak. "I am ready for my retirement," she begins. "I already know what I will do with my time.

"I will volunteer to help at after-school programs.

"I will volunteer at the literacy center to teach adults who cannot read. Reading, we all know, is crucial.

"I will lobby state and local politicians for more money for schools.

"I will go to Washington, D.C., to lobby my congressional representatives. I strongly believe that social justice does not show in the national budget for children's programs.

"Children don't vote," Mrs. Archie continues, "and neither do enough parents. Most people support increasing programs for children, but few organized groups lobby for these programs.

"Did you know that more programs exist for people over sixty-five than for people under six? Think about that," she continues. "In the coming years, raising children will be even more difficult than it is today. It will be especially hard for single parents and for families with both parents working."

Mrs. Archie has a great deal to say about social justice. "In America today, one of every five children is poor. Almost one million—think of that, *one million*—cases of child neglect and child abuse happen every year in this country.

"Social justice begins at home, and in the school, and in our local community. Our country *must* commit more resources to support children and their parents.

"Tonight I am leaving this school as a teacher. I am officially retired, but I do not intend to stop working. I will do what I can to accept the challenges of working for social justice. I urge all of you to do whatever you can, too."

PRACTICE THE SKILLS

A. Vocabulary Skills

1. In the phrase **lobby my congressional representatives,** the word **lobby** means (*a*) elect (*b*) get support from (*c*) defeat (*d*) bring to trial.

2. Which of the following activities would Mrs. Archie probably provide at the **literacy center**? (*a*) arts and crafts (*b*) physical fitness and swimming (*c*) reading and writing (*d*) baking and cooking

3. In the sentence in which the word **anecdote** is used, what is the context clue that tells the meaning of the word **anecdote**?

_____

B. Comprehension Skills

1. Copy one sentence that shows how many years Mrs. Archie taught school.

_____

_____

2. Which of the following awards did Mrs. Archie receive at her retirement? (*a*) key and portrait (*b*) book and poem (*c*) vacation and money (*d*) gift certificates and video

3. Which of the following will NOT occur after her retirement from teaching according to information in the selection? (*a*) trips to Washington (*b*) volunteer at the literacy center (*c*) lobby politicians (*d*) write a book

4. What is the major topic for the minor topics **family, friends,**

   students, community as used in the selection? _____

245

5. Which of the following is the best main idea for the selection?

   (a) Students suffer from lack of support in small town.
   (b) Teachers need to work more hours for kids.
   (c) Retiring teacher will work harder to help children.
   (d) The American family is changing.

6. Probably, the major cause of child neglect is (a) too many programs for the elderly (b) politicians (c) lack of caring teachers (d) single and working parents.

7. **"Children don't vote," Mrs. Archie continues, "and neither do enough parents."** This sentence contains (a) two facts (b) a fact and an opinion (c) two opinions (d) an opinion and a fact.

8. Mrs. Archie thinks that justice means more money for (a) jobs for single mothers (b) teachers' salaries (c) hospitals (d) programs for children.

9. You would think that the best reward Mrs. Archie got from her teaching career was (a) money (b) community recognition (c) personal satisfaction (d) summers off.

10. What does the author think about teachers in general? _____

_____

Explain your answer. _____

_____

C. Study Skills

  1. Complete the following outline with information from the selection.

     I. Mrs. Archie's plans after forty-four years of teaching
       A. Volunteer to help at after-school programs

       B. _____

       C. _____

       D. _____

JUSTICE

II. Four reasons why Mrs. Archie will work to improve the lives of children and families
   A. Children don't vote and neither do enough parents
   B. _____
   C. _____
   D. _____

2. Summarize why you think Mrs. Archie is a good teacher. _____
_____
_____

D. Writing Skills

1. Give two reasons in sentence form why raising a family today is more difficult than in the past.

Reason 1. _____

Reason 2. _____

2. Think of two good reasons why more money should be spent on schools and programs for children. Write at least four sentences.

_____
_____
_____
_____

SELECTION C

How safe do you feel in your community? Perhaps no other issues concern Americans these days as much as violence and crime. How can we make our society a

247

safe place for everyone to live? The problem is very complex.

Let's take a look at some facts about our criminal justice system.

- The United States has some four thousand prisons.
- At any given time, about one and a half million people are incarcerated in these jails.
- Two out of three people who are released from prison will be returned to prison for committing another crime.
- Some ten million Americans have served prison sentences. Most of them are poorly educated and have few job skills.

People who study crime, punishment, and justice in America say that our prison system is both a symptom and a cause of our social sicknesses. These experts agree on one thing: If people who go to jail aren't violent going in, they likely will be violent when they come out. In prisons, human beings live in a degrading lifestyle. We punish them in order to restore and maintain the balance of justice that they upset by committing crimes.

The issue of punishment raises many debatable questions. Should prisoners work in chain gangs (chained together at the ankles) along the sides of American highways? Is this kind of labor an appropriate punishment? Should prisoners who cause trouble be placed in solitary confinement—completely isolated from all others? Should persons sentenced to death be placed on death row?

The most troubling question of all is the issue of capital punishment. Should a person be put to death as punishment for a crime such as murder? Dr. Martin Luther King, Jr., expressed his opinion: "An eye for an eye leaves everybody blind." Today each state decides whether or not to use capital punishment.

PRACTICE THE SKILLS
☑

A. Vocabulary Skills

1. The word **incarcerated** means (*a*) released from jail (*b*) kept in jail (*c*) escaped from jail (*d*) built a jail.

2. The best example of a **degrading lifestyle** in prison is (*a*) being locked into a crowded cell (*b*) being uneducated (*c*) being unemployed (*d*) being ill.

3. **Capital punishment** is decided by (*a*) the president (*b*) individual states (*c*) Martin Luther King (*d*) prisoners.

B. Comprehension Skills

1. Where in the selection can you find factual information about the numbers of jails and prisoners? (*a*) first paragraph (*b*) list in the second paragraph (*c*) fourth paragraph (*d*) last paragraph

2. Who said **"An eye for an eye leaves everybody blind"**?

_____

3. In your own words, tell one fact about released prisoners. Write a complete sentence.

_____

4. The three minor topics from the selection for the major topic **what prison system officials study in America** are (*a*) judges, guards, prisoners (*b*) education, jobs, business (*c*) crime, punishment, justice (*d*) islands, society, weather.

5. Write your own title for this selection using the word **justice.**

_____

6. Solitary confinement is a type of   (*a*) problem in American society today   (*b*) reward for good behavior   (*c*) crime   (*d*) punishment.

7. Copy one fact from the selection about crime that you think deserves the most attention. Then write one opinion of your own telling why you chose that sentence.

_____

_____

8. You would guess that chain gangs are used to   (*a*) get prisoners out of jail early   (*b*) show the public how prisoners can be punished   (*c*) show people why gangs are dangerous   (*d*) improve transportation.

9. What does the author suggest might be the leading cause(s) of crime?   (*a*) lack of education and a good job   (*b*) unfair judges   (*c*) the luxurious prison lifestyle   (*d*) capital punishment

10. The author thinks the prison system in America   (*a*) creates more problems than it solves   (*b*) is extremely successful   (*c*) should adopt capital punishment in every state   (*d*) should name a prison after Martin Luther King.

C. Study Skills

1. Complete the following outline with information from the selection and with your own information.

   I. My four ideas to help solve the problem of crime and improve prisons in America
   A. Prisoners cannot be released until they achieve at least a high school equivalent diploma or extra education

   B. _____

   C. _____

   D. _____

2. Summarize in one sentence what is meant by **"An eye for an eye leaves everybody blind." This quote means** _____

_____

D. Writing Skills

1. Pretend you are in prison. Write one diary entry of at least two sentences.

_____

_____

_____

2. Write at least four sentences explaining why you support or do not support capital punishment. Give at least three reasons for your

answer. _____

_____

_____

_____

Unit Activities

Reread each selection carefully and then complete the following activities independently or in cooperative groups.

Connecting the Theme and Selections

1. **Know.** Tell the example of justice in each selection. The first is done for you.

In Selection A, the example of justice is a family that harassed their neighbors is ordered by the judge to move out of the neighborhood.

In Selection B, _____

_____

In Selection C, _____

_____

2. Comprehend. Explain which selection shows the theme of justice affecting society the most. Give one specific reason for your answer.

_____

_____

_____

3. Apply. Exhibit one picture or drawing of your own that shows justice like that in one of the selections.

4. Analyze. Examine Selections A and B for two reasons each why the family that was harassed in Selection A and Mrs. Archie in Selection B want justice.

Selection A
Reason 1. _____

Reason 2. _____

Selection B
Reason 1. _____

Reason 2. _____

5. Synthesize. Design a specific program for children in school or in their neighborhood that would teach them how to be good neighbors and reduce the possibility of their becoming like the family ordered to move in Selection A.

6. Evaluate. Compare the issue of social justice in Selection B and criminal justice in Selection C. Which one deserves more attention in America? Give three specific reasons for your choice in one well-written paragraph.

Applying the Theme and Selections to the Real World

Use a variety of newspapers, magazines, and other reference materials to complete your choice of the following projects or those assigned to you. Also consider using CD-ROM encyclopedias and other on-line databases as well as television programs and videos to get information for your projects.

Interdisciplinary Project 1

Choose an article in a newspaper about a trial. Write a report that explains the crime that was committed, the verdict in the trial, the punishment for the crime, and whether you think justice was served.

Interdisciplinary Project 2

Research three issues of social justice and three issues of criminal justice. An issue of social justice might be building more homeless shelters. An issue of criminal justice might be parents who abuse their children. Give some examples of how you would show justice for each example.

Interdisciplinary Project 3

Choose a neighbor, teacher, or local official who is involved in trying to improve your neighborhood, school, or city. Interview that person with three to five questions about the key social issues and how the theme of justice fits into that person's actions.

Interdisciplinary Project 4

Read the book *Lord of the Flies* or watch the movie *Papillon.* Explain how either shows a criminal justice system quite different from ours today in America. Do you agree with the system shown? Why or why not?

Interdisciplinary Project 5

Write a short story or poem about someone who is rewarded for doing something good. Include the word *justice* in the story or poem.

UNIT 12

The Theme of
MATURITY

MATURITY is growing up positively.

PREREADING ACTIVITY

1. Think of examples of yourself or someone else that show an act of maturity.

   a. Preparing for a semiformal dinner dance or the senior prom at school
   b. Working part-time during high school or college to pay tuition costs
   c. Doing community service for school or church by volunteering at a homeless shelter

2. Think about why maturity is important in each of the above examples.

   a. Learning about dating and developing social circles of friends
   b. Developing good work habits, savings habits, and spending habits
   c. Improving the community or the quality of life for people less fortunate

3. Now give two examples of your own for maturity and tell why the maturity is important for each example.

A first example is done for you.

Example 1. A high school student becomes an assistant basketball coach for inner-city kids. This allows kids to do organized activities and the student to teach and coach.

Example 2. _____

_____

Example 3. _____

_____

257

SELECTION A

Happy Father's Day, Dad,

I don't know anyone else who deserves more today than you do. You've always tried to make this family the best it can be. I really appreciate all the ways you've helped me.

Thanks, first of all, for giving me all the opportunities for a good education. Your nagging me about being responsible has helped me along the path to maturity. Now I hear your voice in my head asking if I've finished my homework and everything else I'm supposed to do. I really appreciate the long hours you've spent helping me improve my writing.

Most of all, Dad, thanks for the good advice you've given me when I've been in a tough spot.

You've been a great role model for me. Your commitment to your work and your self-discipline baffle me. I honestly don't know how you do it all. I think most other dads come home from work and relax and watch TV and talk to their families. You do that, too, sometimes. But you also have time to coach Little League and be a Crime Watch volunteer and a Big Brother. You show all of us by what you do—not by what you say—that it's important to help people who need help. That's a lesson I won't forget.

Today's the day to thank you for all you've done for me. I just want you to know that I really appreciate your help and guidance. I look forward to all the years ahead of being your son—and of making you proud of me.

I love you.
Chris

PRACTICE THE SKILLS
☑

A. Vocabulary Skills

1. The word **path** in the second paragraph refers to a path traveled (*a*) in life   (*b*) by car   (*c*) by foot   (*d*) in a park.

2. Chris says: **Your commitment to your work and your self-discipline baffle me.** In this sentence, **baffle** means (*a*) frighten (*b*) anger (*c*) please (*d*) amaze.

3. A **role model** is someone who (*a*) earns money by being photographed (*b*) acts in a play (*c*) sets a good example (*d*) teaches in a school.

B. Comprehension Skills

1. In your own words, explain what this sentence means: **You show all of us by what you do—not by what you say.**

_____

_____

_____

2. In what two ways has the father helped his son with his schoolwork?

_____

_____

3. The selection ends with emphasis on the (*a*) past (*b*) present (*c*) future.

4. Two minor topics for the major topic **things that baffle Chris** are (*a*) commitment to work and self-discipline (*b*) writing skills and homework (*c*) income and good education (*d*) unselfish actions and guidance.

5. The best main idea for this selection is (*a*) holidays bring out the best in people (*b*) a son expresses appreciation for his father (*c*) Father's Day is the most important holiday (*d*) parents should help more with schoolwork.

6. What causes Chris to write this letter to his father?

_____

_____

7. The first sentence of the selection is an opinion. Rewrite it into a fact.

_____

_____

8. Chris probably knows a lot about his father's (a) friends (b) work (c) income (d) investments.

9. How would you describe the relationship of the father and son in this selection? (a) excellent (b) good (c) fair (d) poor

10. The author believes that good parenting requires that adults (a) give kids less money to spend (b) plan weekends as a family (c) be good role models (d) become good writers.

C. Study Skills

1. Complete the following outline with information from the selection.

    I. Some reasons why Chris appreciates his father
       A. The never-ending attempt to make the family better

       B. _____

       C. _____

       D. _____

2. Summarize what you think is the best quality of the father and the best quality of the son. **I think the father's best quality is**

_____, **and the son's best quality is** _____.

D. Writing Skills

1. Give one example of advice the father might have given to Chris. Explain Chris's "tough spot" and tell what the father might have advised.

_____

_____

_____

_____

2. Choose a person whom you know and admire. Write at least four sentences to that person. Give specific and mature reasons why you appreciate that person. Use the following format.

Dear _____,

I just wanted to write a few sentences to let you know _____

_____

_____

_____

_____

 SELECTION B

      What's important when you're in elementary school? For many children, priorities are sports and TV, pets, birthday parties, and weekend sleepovers. They don't have to be mature—grown up—until the distant future. They have plenty of time to acquire wisdom and strength.

      But that's not true for one first grader and one third grader at Coastal Ridge Elementary School in York, Maine. Both have had to face life-and-death issues. Both are afflicted with cancer and are receiving treatment for the disease. Their illnesses have affected the whole school. Students have responded by bringing some brightness into the lives of the school's students, their parents, the staff, and the entire community.

In an effort to raise awareness about cancer, Coastal Ridge students created a Kids Cabinet. This core group of seventeen students has organized events to raise money for cancer awareness projects in the school and in the community. They have donated some of the money they raised to the Maine Children's Cancer Program.

One of the projects of the Kids Cabinet is a video titled "Caring for Others." This video gives questions and answers about cancer topics. It explains various treatments for the disease. On the video, students interview their two classmates who have cancer. The two girls, aged seven and nine, explain that a series of chemotherapy treatments causes hair loss and fatigue. They vow to become healthy and cured in the years ahead.

The video ends with a song sung by the entire school. The final lyrics are, "We are the children of tomorrow. It's all up to us to find a better way." Such a level of maturity is quite remarkable for children who are just learning how to read and write, ride a bike, and hit a baseball.

PRACTICE THE SKILLS

A. Vocabulary Skills

1. **Priorities** are things that are (a) expensive (b) not important (c) important (d) dangerous.

2. In the phrase **acquire wisdom and strength,** the word **acquire** means (a) lose (b) gain (c) buy (d) destroy.

3. In the phrase **afflicted with cancer,** which of the following phrases uses the word **afflicted** correctly? (*a*) afflicted with knowledge (*b*) afflicted with skills (*c*) afflicted with pleasure (*d*) afflicted with pain

B. Comprehension Skills

1. Write the sentence that answers the question, **What's important when you're in elementary school?** _____

_____

2. What was the name of the core group that organized the projects? (*a*) Coastal Ridge (*b*) Kids Cabinet (*c*) Caring for Others (*d*) Maine Children's Cancer Program

3. Which of the following events happens first? (*a*) hair loss (*b*) fatigue (*c*) chemotherapy treatment (*d*) cancer is cured

4. The major topic for the minor topics **read, write, ride a bike, hit a baseball** is (*a*) things students do in the video (*b*) things students learn to do (*c*) things that prove maturity (*d*) things that raised funds.

5. Write a one-sentence main idea for the entire selection using the words **kids, maturity,** and **cancer.** _____

6. According to the selection, the only difference between the two girls with cancer is their (*a*) age and grade (*b*) level of maturity (*c*) number of absences from school (*d*) number of friends.

7. Is the following sentence fact or opinion? **This core group of seventeen students has organized events to raise money for cancer awareness projects.** _____

8. Which of the following seem to have done the most work to bring cancer awareness to the school and community? (*a*) parents (*b*) students (*c*) teachers (*d*) hospital officials

9. The final lyrics of the song on the video express students' (*a*) fear of the future (*b*) willingness to help others (*c*) understanding of cancer treatments (*d*) understanding of history.

10. The author's main purpose in writing this selection is to show (*a*) how good our schools are today (*b*) how hospitals get money for research (*c*) why television is a good teaching tool (*d*) what can cause kids to act like adults.

C. Study Skills

1. Complete the following outline with information from the selection.

I. Cancer awareness projects at Coastal Ridge Elementary School

  A. Created Kids Cabinet

  B. _____

    1. Questions and answers about cancer topics

    2. _____

    3. _____

  C. _____

II. Some effects of chemotherapy

  A. _____

  B. _____

III. What the girls vow to do

  A. _____

  B. _____

2. Summarize the lyrics of the song sung by the students. **The song is about** _____

_____

D. Writing Skills

1. The students in this selection undertook some projects to show their concern for the two girls with cancer. Think of three other situations that might cause students to undertake projects to help others. Write one sentence for each situation.

   Example: Students help a family whose home was destroyed by fire.

   _____

   _____

   _____

   _____

2. Now choose one of the situations you described in question 1. Describe three specific projects that students could do to help the people in that situation. Write at least three sentences.

   _____

   _____

   _____

   _____

   _____

   _____

 SELECTION C

One of the qualities of maturity is being able to communicate well at home, in school, at work, and among friends. You use four major communication skills: listening, speaking, reading, and writing. These four skills are listed in the order of most frequent use. On average, you listen more often than you speak, you speak more than you read, and you read more than you write.

Experts have identified four different types of speaking and listening and the purpose of each.

- First, there is *phatic communication*. Phatic speaking and listing involves small talk, such as talk about the weather, how the local team did in the game last night, or your plans for the weekend. Phatic listening shows the speaker that you are interested in communicating. It also allows for possible movement up the ladder of communication.
- Second on that ladder of speaking and listening skills is *cathartic communication*. When you are using cathartic listening, you are listening to a speaker talk about his or her problems or needs. This type of listening shows that you care about what the speaker has to say. It helps to develop trust between speaker and listener.
- *Listening for information* is the third step or purpose on the speaking and listening ladder. When you listen for information, you make decisions or take actions based on what you hear. You might listen for directions on how to get somewhere or listen to political candidates stating their views.
- The fourth and highest level of communication is *persuasion*. It's one thing to chat about the weather or a good movie you saw (phatic communication) or listen to a friend's problem at school or work (cathartic communication). Persuasion is quite another thing. Persuasion involves decision making based on information. You are involved in persuasion when you discuss a point of view in a school debate or when you decide which college to attend or which house to buy after you begin a career.

The third and fourth levels of communication—information and persuasion—require the most skill. They are also the most important communication skills used in school and at work.

To become a more mature and effective communicator, you need to feel comfortable speaking and listening at each level. You also need to be aware of your purpose. Finally, you need to balance the use of phatic, cathartic, information, and persuasion communication in your daily routine. If you never move beyond the small talk of phatic communication, you are missing a great deal.

PRACTICE THE SKILLS

A. Vocabulary Skills

1. **Phatic** and **cathartic** are two kinds of   (*a*) careers   (*b*) books   (*c*) communication   (*d*) weather.

2. **Persuasion** usually requires you to   (*a*) take a test   (*b*) speak before a group   (*c*) get a better education   (*d*) make a decision.

3. In the following sentence, what does the word **chat** mean? **It's one thing to chat about the weather or a good movie you saw.**
   (*a*) give information   (*b*) talk   (*c*) persuade   (*d*) make a decision

B. Comprehension Skills

1. What are the four major skills in communicating? _____

   _____

   _____

2. The two most important kinds of listening skills in school or work are   (*a*) phatic and cathartic   (*b*) information and persuasion   (*c*) phatic and information   (*d*) cathartic and information.

3. An example of persuasion is   (*a*) getting to know a new friend
(*b*) listening to a salesperson trying to sell you a car   (*c*) listening to
directions for taking a test   (*d*) explaining to a friend how you feel
about a problem.

4. What is the communication purpose in talking to a doctor about
your symptoms of an illness, talking to a mechanic about something
wrong with your car, talking to a librarian about sources for a
research paper? (*a*) phatic   (*b*) cathartic   (*c*) information
(*d*) persuasion

5. Which of the following is the best title for this selection?
(*a*) The Importance of Speaking and Listening Effectively
(*b*) The History of Communication
(*c*) How to Use the Computer for Improved Communication
(*d*) Why Writing and Reading Are Important During Communication

6. Good communication skills are probably needed most to keep
(*a*) good health   (*b*) a good job   (*c*) good friends   (*d*) good vacations.

7. Which of the following is a fact that could introduce the selection?
(*a*) All adults are mature.
(*b*) All adults have good qualities.
(*c*) All adults need to communicate.
(*d*) All adults have good jobs.

8. Writing is the communication skill that is   (*a*) used most often
(*b*) used least often   (*c*) most important in decision making
(*d*) most important in gathering information.

9. Overall, the most important type of communication skill seems to be
(*a*) writing   (*b*) reading   (*c*) speaking   (*d*) listening.

Explain your answer. _____

_____

10. The author thinks that you need to know how to   (*a*) discuss the weather and movies   (*b*) become a good listener   (*c*) get into college (*d*) invest money wisely.

C. Study Skills

1. Complete the following outline with information from the selection.
  I. Four types of communication
    A. Writing

    B. _____

    C. _____

    D. _____

  II. Four purposes of communication and one example of each
    A. Phatic—small talk
      1. The weather

    B. Cathartic—_____

      1. _____

    C. _____

      1. _____

    D. _____

      1. _____

2. Summarize why developing good speaking and listening skills is so important. Give at least two reasons in the following format. **Good**

speaking and listening skills are important because _____

_____

_____

_____

D. Writing Skills

1. Choose two of the four purposes of communicating. For each purpose that you choose, write a sentence that gives an example of that type of communication. An example is done for you.

Example 1. Phatic. Those shoes look very comfortable and go well with that suit.

Example 2. _____

Example 3. _____

2. Imagine that you are trying to persuade a fellow student to buy your used mountain bike or to join the school newspaper staff. Use both information and persuasion as you try to convince the student. Write at least four sentences.

_____

_____

_____

_____

_____

_____

Unit Activities

Reread each selection carefully and then complete the following activities independently or in cooperative groups.

Connecting the Theme and Selections

1. **Know.** Name the situation in each selection that shows the theme of maturity. The first is done for you.

MATURITY

In Selection A, the theme of maturity is shown by a boy writing a Father's Day letter and expressing his thanks for all that his father has done for him.

In Selection B, _____

_____

_____

In Selection C, _____

_____

_____

2. **Comprehend.** Compare the two selections that are most alike in terms of the theme of maturity and give two reasons for your choices.

3. **Apply.** Explain two major communication skills from Selection C that are used to show the theme of maturity in Selections A and B. Your choices are writing, reading, speaking, and listening skills.

4. **Analyze.** Arrange the four communication skills from Selection C in order from the one you use most to the one you use least.

   1. _____

   2. _____

   3. _____

   4. _____

5. **Synthesize.** Imagine that you are writing an interview with one of the girls in Selection B. Write questions and answers that include the four purposes: phatic, cathartic, information, persuasion. With a classmate, try to audiotape or videotape the interview.

6. Evaluate. Decide who is more mature, the boy in Selection A or the two girls with cancer in Selection B. Give at least three reasons in the following format.

I think that _____ in Selection ____ shows more maturity.

Reason 1. _____

Reason 2. _____

Reason 3. _____

Applying the Theme and Selections to the Real World

Use a variety of newspapers, magazines, and other reference materials to complete your choice of the following projects or those assigned to you. Also consider using CD-ROM encyclopedias and other on-line databases as well as television programs and videos to get information for your projects.

Interdisciplinary Project 1

Read a major newspaper. Choose five articles that you think show the theme of maturity the best. Rank your articles 1 to 5 with best example of maturity first. After each, write two or three sentences summarizing what the article is about, how it shows maturity, and why you chose it.

Interdisciplinary Project 2

Create a collage of your own five original drawings and/or poems from your own observations of maturity in the daily routine of your school, work, and/or neighborhood.

Interdisciplinary Project 3

Research a child or young adult in present or recent history who has demonstrated the theme of maturity. Complete a report of several paragraphs with pictures, if available.

Interdisciplinary Project 4

Design your own Father's and/or Mother's Day card and a Get Well and/or Friendship card aligned with the theme of maturity shown in Selections A and B.

Interdisciplinary Project 5

Watch a thirty-minute television program. Create a checklist of each time you listen to phatic, cathartic, information, and persuasion statements. Then summarize your conclusions about the purposes for speaking and listening as described in Selection C.

UNIT 13

The Theme of

MOTIVATION

Definition

MOTIVATION is the reason or influence that causes you to do something.

PREREADING ACTIVITY

1. We are constantly doing things or watching other people doing things. Think about examples of people doing routine things.

   a. Doing homework
   b. Painting your house
   c. Helping an elderly neighbor clean the yard

2. Think about different reasons that cause someone to do these things.

   a. Wanting good grades or being punished for not completing assignments
   b. Keeping property in good condition or preparing to sell the house
   c. Wanting to help someone in need or to make some money

3. Now give two examples of your own for motivation and tell at least two different reasons or causes for doing each.

A *first example is done for you.*

Example 1. Making friends with a new student or coworker to make him or her feel welcome.

Example 2. _____

_____

Example 3. _____

_____

SELECTION A

Every day you take many actions. You choose how long to study for a test, how to react to new students, what to do with your free time. Do you have any idea what your motives, or reasons for behavior, are?

Understanding why people—including yourself—act the way they do is an important part of your education. An awareness of motivations not only helps improve your relationships, but also helps you understand yourself better.

There are two basic types of motivation: intrinsic and extrinsic motivation. To help you remember which is which, think of the words *internal* (inside) and *external* (outside).

Intrinsic motivation is internal. The reason for doing something comes from within. In other words, you do something because you want to. The motive for your action is not money or a prize. Rather, the reward is being part of something or the accomplishment itself, or just getting a sincere thank-you.

Here are some examples of actions with intrinsic motivations:

- A grandfather takes his granddaughter to the zoo because he enjoys seeing her happy.
- A Little League coach spends time in practice and at games because he likes baseball so much and enjoys helping young students.
- A doctor cares for children in a poor rural area because she wants to help them live healthier lives.

Extrinsic motivations are external. They come from outside yourself. For example, you might take a certain action because you hope to win money, a prize, a promotion, or some kind of power or prestige. Here are some other examples:

- Jana tries hard to make the honor roll because all honor roll students receive a discount at the local record store.
- A basketball player leaves college to play with the pros. He signs a two-year multimillion-dollar contract with a professional team.
- An executive leaves a small company that helped pay her way through college. She takes a job with a big company that gives her a promotion, a bigger salary, and a company car.

In each of the preceding examples, the motivation is some form of money and/or advancement. While we need to earn money and advance in our jobs, we also need to do things just for personal satisfaction. A good balance of intrinsic and extrinsic motivation is probably best.

What are some of the reasons why you do some of the things you do?

PRACTICE THE SKILLS

A. Vocabulary Skills

1. If you mow your neighbor's lawn while he is in the hospital, the motivation is   (*a*) intrinsic   (*b*) extrinsic.

If you mow your neighbor's lawn only if he pays you twenty dollars, the motivation is   (*a*) intrinsic   (*b*) extrinsic.

2. The word in the selection that means the same as **motive** is (*a*) type   (*b*) reason   (*c*) relationship   (*d*) accomplishment.

3. In the phrase **some kind of power or prestige,** the word **prestige** could be replaced with the word   (*a*) respect   (*b*) contract (*c*) company   (*d*) thank-you.

B. Comprehension Skills

1. Why did the executive leave the smaller company for the bigger company? (*a*) free college tuition (*b*) bigger salary and company car (*c*) family and friends could get jobs (*d*) multimillion-dollar contract

2. How many major types of motivation are described in the selection? (*a*) two (*b*) three (*c*) four (*d*) five

3. Which of the following is an example of extrinsic motivation? (*a*) Sheryl works for hours in the garden because she likes gardening. (*b*) Paolo is reading a book by his favorite author. (*c*) Mrs. Yin works overtime to earn more money. (*d*) Mr. Kramer studies Russian because he enjoys learning a language.

4. The major topic for the minor topics **money, prize, promotion** is (*a*) rewards (*b*) self-satisfaction (*c*) rural things (*d*) favors.

5. The best main idea for the selection is
(*a*) how parents can motivate children
(*b*) how to understand the motivation in a person's actions
(*c*) how to prepare students to do better in school
(*d*) how sports teams win championships

6. Something that is done for an intrinsic reason usually makes you feel (*a*) poor (*b*) good (*c*) rich (*d*) very bad.

7. Would you classify the following statement as a fact or an opinion? **A good balance of intrinsic and extrinsic motivation is probably best.** (*a*) opinion (*b*) fact

8. You would think that learning about motivation is accomplished (*a*) mostly in college (*b*) mostly in work (*c*) over a long period of time (*d*) mostly in sports.

9. You would think that a very important skill as a parent, coach, teacher, or boss is (*a*) developing extrinsic motivations (*b*) offering money for good deeds (*c*) getting politicians on your side (*d*) expecting a balance of intrinsic and extrinsic motivations.

10. The author's purpose in writing this selection is to give
(*a*) directions   (*b*) information   (*c*) opinions   (*d*) solutions.

C. Study Skills

1. Complete the following outline with information from the selection.

    I. Some examples of intrinsic motivation
      A. Grandfather takes granddaughter to the zoo

      B. _____

      C. _____

    II. Some examples of extrinsic motivation

      A. _____

      B. _____

      C. _____

2. Summarize the major difference between intrinsic motivation and

extrinsic motivation. _____

_____

_____

_____

D. Writing Skills

1. Give one specific example of intrinsic motivation and one specific

example of extrinsic motivation that you have observed. _____

_____

_____

2. Give one example of something you recently did that was intrinsically motivated and one thing you did that was extrinsically motivated. What were the "rewards" for each? Which one did you enjoy the most? Why? Write at least four sentences.

_____

_____

_____

_____

 SELECTION B

Khalid Omalek has been in America for seven years. He works as a dishwasher. He grew up in Casablanca, Morocco. "God bless America," he tells his classmates.

Jean Estime immigrated to America from the poverty of Haiti in 1983. A housepainter, Estime thanks his many teachers for their hard work.

Anthony Maffei, Mark Manns, and Gerry Raymond grew up together in the same neighborhood in Sacramento. As teenagers, they dropped out of high school. All work odd jobs as laborers. They were mistaken, they know now, to think that somehow success can be achieved without work.

For these students, tonight is graduation night. They are ABE (Adult Basic Education) students at the SCALE school in Sacramento, California. (SCALE stands for Sacramento Adult Learning Experience.) Twenty-eight students will receive certificates for completing their SCALE courses. Most will go on to work toward their high school diplomas. Some of the graduates express a desire to then go on to college.

These SCALE graduates are success stories, ranging in age from twenty-two to sixty-two. They are highly motivated students from diverse backgrounds. Their goals are simple: to become literate (able to read and write), to be a role model for their children, and to get a good job. They found their 6 P.M. to 9 P.M. classes difficult but rewarding.

The biggest success story this year is the keynote speaker at graduation, Amelia Susi. Amelia came to America from Albania in 1971. She married and had two children. During the 1970s, she took ABE courses and graduated. Throughout the 1980s, she took the equivalent of four years of high school night courses at SCALE. She received her high school diploma in 1988. Two years later, she realized her life-long dream. She opened Amelia's Kitchen, one of Sacramento's most popular neighborhood restaurants. Her current plans, she tells the graduates, include college courses in business and marketing.

All across America on any given weekday evening, adult students are attending ABE classes. Most are high school dropouts. One can only marvel at their desire to learn. After working a full-time job all day, they study and attend classes at night. They must pass the free ABE courses before enrolling in a high school diploma program. Most ABE students need reading, writing, and public speaking skills, not to mention a good dose of self-esteem and a pat on the back.

These students illustrate the great power of motivation. For them, hard work, determination, and a lot of motivation open the doors of opportunity.

PRACTICE THE SKILLS

A. Vocabulary Skills

1. In the sentence **One can only marvel at their desire to learn,** the word **marvel** means to be   (a) concerned   (b) impressed   (c) hurt   (d) paid.

2. The best word to replace the word **enrolling** in the phrase **enrolling in a high school diploma program** is   (a) reading   (b) graduating   (c) registering   (d) living.

3. In the phrase **students from diverse backgrounds,** the word **diverse** could be replaced with the word   (*a*) alike   (*b*) unknown   (*c*) different   (*d*) religious.

B. Comprehension Skills

1. Who was the keynote speaker?   (*a*) Khalid Omalek   (*b*) Anthony Maffei   (*c*) Gerry Raymond   (*d*) Amelia Susi

2. Most of the students worked during the day as   (*a*) laborers   (*b*) teachers   (*c*) businesspeople   (*d*) government officials.

3. Before enrolling at SCALE, a student must first   (*a*) take some college courses   (*b*) pass some ABE courses   (*c*) work a full-time job   (*d*) own a business.

4. The major topic for the minor topics **become literate, be a role model, get a good job** is   (*a*) courses offered at the school   (*b*) reading, writing, and public speaking skills   (*c*) goals of SCALE students   (*d*) reasons why people come to America.

5. Write your own title for this selection. Include some form of the word **motivation.**

_____

6. The major differences of the students are   (*a*) age and nationality   (*b*) number of children and marital status   (*c*) athletic abilities and hobbies   (*d*) kind of car and home.

7. Copy one fact about one of the students in the selection. _____

_____

Now rewrite that fact into an opinion. _____

_____

_____

8. Thus far, you would guess that which person has benefited most from the courses at SCALE?   (a) Jean Estime   (b) Mark Manns   (c) Amelia Susi   (d) none of these

Explain your answer. _____

_____

_____

9. The problem that most students seem to experience in the SCALE program is finding   (a) money for the courses   (b) good teachers   (c) enough books   (d) times to study and attend classes.

10. Does the author support adult education classes?   (a) yes   (b) no

Explain your answer. _____

_____

_____

C. Study Skills

1. Complete the following outline with information from the selection.

I. Goals of SCALE students
A. Become literate

B. _____

C. _____

II. Names and background information of some currently graduating students
A. Khalid Omalek is a dishwasher from Morocco

B. _____

C. _____

III. _____

    A. Keynote speaker for the graduation

    B. _____

    C. _____

    D. _____

    E. _____

    F. Her current plans include college courses in business and marketing

2. Summarize in one sentence why Khalid Omalek said "God bless America."

_____

_____

D. Writing Skills

1. If you were a teacher in the SCALE program, write the first sentence you would say to your new class on the first night. _____

_____

2. Write the first four or five sentences of the speech that you would give at the graduation if you were Amelia Susi. _____

_____

_____

_____

_____

_____

SELECTION C

Jessica Dubroff wanted to "fly till I die." And she did.

At four feet two inches, and weighing fifty-five pounds, Jessica Dubroff sat in the pilot's seat of a Cessna 177B. This second grader had to have blocks on the pedals so her feet could reach the rudder controls.

Jessica Dubroff's story provides a lesson about motivation gone wrong. She wanted to be the youngest pilot in aviation history to fly across the United States. From San Diego to Boston, her photos adorned the front pages of newspapers. Her parents and her flight instructor had talk show interviews lined up. Book and movie rights to Jessica's story were being discussed. Profits were on the horizon.

But what was billed as a simple father-daughter adventure quickly got out of hand. The media blitz prompted her cross-country trek. The Federal Aviation Administration (FAA) had no rules to prohibit youngsters from flying a plane as long as a certified flight instructor was aboard.

Jessica, her father, and a flight instructor set out from San Diego. The first leg of their cross-country journey was California to Wyoming, and it was successful. But the second leg ended tragically.

On a cold April morning, Jessica attempted a takeoff into the thin air above the Rocky Mountains. The plane was overloaded. Several seconds after takeoff, the Cessna nosedived into a Wyoming highway. Jessica, her father, and her flight instructor were killed.

FAA officials blamed the weather conditions and ice on the plane's wings as the likely cause of the crash. Her mother said, "She died doing what she enjoyed."

Outrage and debate followed the crash. Some people said that the three deaths had been caused by adults allowing children to have too much freedom. Adults allowed children to pursue enjoyment in the face of danger, they said. Adults had become foolishly caught up in the glamour of instant stardom.

Jessica Dubroff's story is a lesson about motivation and common sense. Unfortunately, it is a lesson learned the hard way.

MOTIVATION

PRACTICE THE SKILLS
☑

A. Vocabulary Skills

1. The best synonym for **outrage** is   (a) fear   (b) sadness   (c) absence   (d) anger.

2. **She wanted to be the youngest pilot in aviation history to fly across the United States.** In this sentence, the best context clue that tells about the meaning of **aviation** is   (a) Jessica   (b) fly   (c) history   (d) United States.

3. The word **leg** as used in the selection is refers to   (a) a part of the body   (b) a nickname   (c) food   (d) distance.

B. Comprehension Skills

1. Which paragraphs contain information about the crash and the causes?   (a) first and second   (b) first and third   (c) third and fourth   (d) six and seventh

2. Who died in the crash along with Jessica?   (a) father and mother   (b) mother and news reporter   (c) father and flight instructor   (d) parents and flight instructor

3. Which of the following is the correct sequence of events in the selection?
   (a) flew from California, landed in Wyoming, crashed after takeoff from Wyoming
   (b) flew to California, flew to Wyoming, crashed in Boston
   (c) took off from Boston, flew to Wyoming, crashed after takeoff from California
   (d) none of these

4. What are the three minor topics in the selection for the major topic

   possible sources of profit from the flight? _____

5. The phrase that makes the best title for this selection is   (*a*) one spring morning   (*b*) fly till I die   (*c*) aviation   (*d*) attempting a takeoff.

6. During Jessica's cross-country flight, the flight conditions in California and Wyoming were different because of the   (*a*) size of the airport   (*b*) amount of air traffic   (*c*) lack of people to repair the plane   (*d*) weather.

7. Most of the facts in the selection are about   (*a*) people and events   (*b*) time and places   (*c*) television and newspaper stories   (*d*) airports and government agencies.

8. All of the following people could have somehow prevented the accident EXCEPT   (*a*) FAA officials   (*b*) parents   (*c*) flight instructor   (*d*) talk show hosts.

9. Do you agree or disagree with Jessica's mother's statement, **"She died doing what she enjoyed"**? In other words, do you think

Jessica enjoyed what she was doing? _____

_____

10. The author is biased against people who   (*a*) allow children to miss school   (*b*) use children for profit   (*c*) force children to fly rather than drive   (*d*) fly private airplanes.

C. Study Skills

1. Complete the following outline with your own information and information from the selection.

   I. Some reasons why her parents wanted Jessica to complete the flight

      A. _____

      B. _____

      C. _____

MOTIVATION

II. Some reasons why the crash occurred

   A. _____

   B. _____

   C. _____

III. Some public reactions to the crash

   A. _____

   B. _____

   C. _____

2. In your own words, tell what you think this sentence means: **Unfortunately, it is a lesson learned the hard way.**

   _____

   _____

D. Writing Skills

1. Write the first sentence of a newspaper story about Jessica's plane crash. In your sentence answer all of these questions: Who? What happened? Where? When?

   _____

2. Write a letter to the director of the FAA (Federal Aviation Administration). Urge the director to make new rules that will prohibit children from flying airplanes. Write at least four sentences. State your opinion clearly and give facts to support it.

   _____

   _____

   _____

   _____

MOTIVATION

Unit Activities

Reread each selection carefully and then complete the following activities independently or in cooperative groups.

Connecting the Theme and Selections

1. **Know.** Identify three examples of motivation from each selection. A first from each selection is done for you.

Selection A

Example 1. An executive changes companies to get a promotion, a bigger salary, and a company car.

Example 2. _____

Example 3. _____

Selection B

Example 1. Students attend adult education classes to become literate, become role models for their children, and get good jobs.

Example 2. _____

Example 3. _____

Selection C

Example 1. Jessica Dubroff wanted to become the youngest pilot in history to fly across the United States.

Example 2. _____

Example 3. _____

2. **Comprehend.** Identify one example of intrinsic motivation and one example of extrinsic motivation in each selection and give the "reward" for each. You may use examples from *Know* above. An example of each type of motivation is provided.

In Selection A, the doctor is intrinsically motivated to work with children in poor rural areas because the reward is helping children in need.

In Selection A, the executive is extrinsically motivated to change jobs because the reward is a promotion, more money, and a company car.

MOTIVATION

Selection A

Intrinsic motivation and reward. ———————————————————

Extrinsic motivation and reward. ———————————————————

Selection B

Intrinsic motivation and reward. ———————————————————

Extrinsic motivation and reward. ———————————————————

Selection C

Intrinsic motivation and reward. ———————————————————

Extrinsic motivation and reward. ———————————————————

3. **Apply.** Illustrate one example of intrinsic and one example of extrinsic motivation in the three selections with drawings of your own or pictures from the media.

4. **Analyze.** Summarize the best example of intrinsic and the best example of extrinsic motivation from the three selections. Explain the reason for your choice of each. Think about the number of people affected by each example as a basis of your choice.

Best example of intrinsic motivation. ———————————————

Reason. ———————————————————————————————

Best example of extrinsic motivation. ———————————————

Reason. ———————————————————————————————

5. **Synthesize.** Compose a song about intrinsic and extrinsic motivation with lyrics that support a balance of the two types and examples of each. Include the rewards that go with them. You may use the examples in the three selections or make up examples of your own.

6. **Evaluate.** Predict the next situation in which your motivation will be intrinsic and the next situation in which it will be extrinsic. Describe the cause of the motivation and the possible reward.

MOTIVATION

Applying the Theme and Selections to the Real World

Use a variety of newspapers, magazines, and other reference materials to complete your choice of the following projects or those assigned to you. Also consider using CD-ROM encyclopedias and other on-line databases as well as television programs and videos to get information for your projects.

Interdisciplinary Project 1

Research the story of Daedalus and his son, Icarus. Compare and contrast this famous myth with the story of Jessica Dubroff and her father. Complete a written report with drawings or pictures that show both sets of people and the respective stories.

Interdisciplinary Project 2

Create a collage of five examples of intrinsic motivation and five examples of extrinsic motivation. Be sure to label, describe, and give the reward for each motivation or action.

Interdisciplinary Project 3

Write a report about a famous person in present or past history. Explain what he or she did. Also explain what motivated that person's actions and give a few examples. What were the rewards for the actions?

Interdisciplinary Project 4

Create an outline or journal of examples of intrinsic motivation and extrinsic motivation that you observe over a period of several days. Include the actions, the causes of the actions, and the rewards.

Interdisciplinary Project 5

Interview the owner of a company. Develop three to five questions about motivation and rewards that the owner uses to improve the business and keep it successful. Also give information about the owner's types and examples of motivation.

UNIT 14

The Theme of
SURVIVAL

SURVIVAL is the ability to stay alive or to live longer than others.

PREREADING ACTIVITY

1. Have you heard about a person surviving a car accident or a fire? What are some of the reasons why a person survives a car accident? Why do some people not survive a car accident?

2. Also think about other natural disasters involving survival, such as hurricanes and floods. What causes some people to survive a hurricane, while others do not?

3. Now think about survival in terms of such things as a basketball tournament or a job interview or a disease.

Explain how the word **survive** relates to each example in 3 above with a sentence of your own for each of the following.

A first example is done for you.

Example. In a basketball tournament, the winning team survives or moves on to play the next game, while the tournament ends for the losing team.

A job interview. _____

_____

A disease. _____

_____

4. Finally, give two examples of your own for survival. Then write a short explanation of how surviving (or not surviving) applies to your example.

A first example is done for you.

Example. A rollerblader has a bad spill but is spared serious injury because of a crash helmet.

Example 1. _____

_____

Example 2. _____

_____

SELECTION A

Jack Newcomb froze in horror. Not many things frighten Big Jack. (They call him Big Jack because he is six feet six inches tall.) But he was staring at a three-foot-long snake hanging from his right hand—a snake with rattles on its tail. The snake's fangs were sunk in Jack's hand.

He had been looking for an old shovel in the corner of his garage. When he reached behind a box of books, the rattlesnake struck. Its fangs punched two tiny, deadly holes in his hand. In a second, a stream of venom shot into Jack's hand. In another split second, Jack shook the snake loose. Quickly, it slithered away.

Jack yelled to his wife, "Call 911! A rattlesnake bit me!"

The paramedics arrived just six minutes later, but to Jack the wait seemed like six hours. Luckily, he remembered his first-aid training:

298

- First, wrap a cloth tightly between the snakebite and the heart.
- Second, stay calm.
- Third, breathe very slowly.

These three steps keep snake venom from spreading quickly through the body. Jack found a rag in the garage and wrapped it tightly above his wrist. He sat down and tried to wait calmly.

When the EMTs (emergency medical technicians) arrived, Jack could hardly see them. His vision had already blurred. His hand was badly swollen, and the pain was intense.

The paramedics rushed Jack to the nearest hospital. Almost immediately, a doctor gave him an antivenom shot to fight the rattlesnake poison. Before the antivenom started working, Jack's heart almost stopped several times. He was close to dying.

Big Jack Newcomb knows that he is a lucky man. The pain and swelling lasted for several weeks, but he survived. He likes to tell his story about the rattler that bit and got away.

PRACTICE THE SKILLS

A. Vocabulary Skills

1. The word **fangs** as used in the selection best refers to   (a) hands   (b) feet   (c) teeth   (d) legs.

2. Rewrite the following sentence, replacing the word **venom** with a new word of your own. **These three steps keep snake venom from spreading quickly through the body.**

_____

_____

3. What word in the selection means the same as **paramedic**?
(*a*) antivenom   (*b*) swelling   (*c*) emergency   (*d*) EMT

B. Comprehension Skills

1. Where does this story take place?   (*a*) a garage   (*b*) a school   (*c*) a hospital   (*d*) a zoo. Copy the sentence that proves your answer.

_____

2. How long did it take paramedics to arrive at the scene?   (*a*) about six minutes   (*b*) about six hours   (*c*) about six days   (*d*) they never arrived

3. What happened immediately after the snake bit Jack?   (*a*) It slithered away.   (*b*) His wife called 911.   (*c*) Jack had blurred vision.   (*d*) Jack shook the snake loose.

4. The minor topics **box of books** and **old shovel** as used in the selection have the major topic   (*a*) things Jack used to hit the snake   (*b*) things stored in Jack's garage   (*c*) things the snake knocked over   (*d*) none of these.

5. Use information from the selection to complete the following sentence in your own words. **The main idea of this story is** _____

_____

_____

6. What do you think caused the snake to bite Jack? _____

_____

Could he have avoided being bitten? _____

How? _____

_____

7. How would you describe most of the information in this selection? (*a*) mostly facts (*b*) mostly opinions (*c*) about the same number of facts as opinions

Explain your answer. _____

_____

8. Why did Jack wrap a rag tightly above his wrist? (*a*) to reduce the pain (*b*) to keep himself breathing (*c*) to kill the snake (*d*) to slow the venom from spreading

9. You would reason that Jack survived the snakebite because (*a*) he was smart (*b*) help arrived soon (*c*) his wife helped (*d*) all of these.

10. The author probably believes that Jack is (*a*) clumsy (*b*) quick thinking (*c*) slow (*d*) foolish.

C. Study Skills

1. Complete the following outline with information from the selection.

    I. _____

        A. First, wrap a cloth tightly between the snakebite and the heart
        B. Second, stay calm

        C. _____

2. Summarize the events in the story in one sentence. _____

_____

D. Writing Skills

1. Write the first sentence that you think Jack's wife spoke when she called 911.

_____

_____

2. Write a four- to seven-sentence paragraph that gives instructions for avoiding a snakebite and what to do if bitten by a poisonous snake. Use information from the selection in your paragraph.

_____

_____

_____

_____

 SELECTION B

A Maryland commuter train bound for Union Station in Washington, D.C., crashed into a freight train heading in the same direction. The commuter train erupted in a ball of flames on a snow-swept stretch of track. The accident happened yesterday at 7:45 A.M. during the morning rush hour.

The four-car commuter train was carrying 150 passengers. At least twelve people died, and dozens were injured. All of the deaths and the worst of the injuries occurred on the commuter train. Most of the victims were trapped in the first car. The commuter train's doors did not open automatically upon impact, as they were supposed to do.

Moments before the impact, two conductors raced through the commuter train to warn the passengers of the impending accident. The engineer had seen the freight train directly ahead on the same track. He knew there was not enough time to stop. (At sixty to seventy miles per hour, trains need about one minute or one mile to stop.)

One survivor said she thought that the commuter train was on the wrong track. It had changed tracks about ten minutes before the crash.

Officials believe that the commuter train's engineer

may have missed a yellow signal. Instead of slowing the train, the engineer kept going at full speed.

A full investigation is underway.

PRACTICE THE SKILLS

A. Vocabulary Skills

1. The word **erupted** as used in the phrase **erupted in a ball of flames** best relates to   (a) an explosion   (b) a rescue   (c) the weather   (d) a sports event.

2. The word **bound** as used in the selection means   (a) returning from   (b) remaining in   (c) heading for   (d) tied up.

3. Rewrite the following sentence, replacing the italicized words with new words of your own: **Moments before the *impact*, two conductors raced through the commuter train to warn the passengers of the *impending* accident.**

_____

_____

B. Comprehension Skills

1. Copy the sentence that tells where most of the victims were seated during the accident. _____

_____

2. How much distance does it take for a train to stop when it is moving about sixty to seventy miles per hour?   (a) one-quarter mile   (b) one-half mile   (c) one mile   (d) two miles

303

SURVIVAL

3. What happened a moment before the accident?   (*a*) The car doors opened.   (*b*) The conductors warned the passengers.   (*c*) The commuter train increased speed.   (*d*) The freight train changed tracks.

4. Under the major topic **types of trains,** what are the two minor topics from the selection? _____

5. Write a title for this selection. _____

6. The effect of the train's doors not opening automatically probably caused   (*a*) more people to die   (*b*) fewer people to die   (*c*) everyone to die   (*d*) no difference in the number of deaths.

Explain your answer. _____

_____

7. In your own words, write a factual statement about the train accident.

_____

_____

Now write an opinion about the events in this selection.

_____

_____

8. You would draw the conclusion that a commuter train transports   (*a*) people   (*b*) machinery   (*c*) livestock   (*d*) food.

9. You would reason that the most important survivor with accurate information about the accident is the   (*a*) conductor   (*b*) freight train engineer   (*c*) frequent passenger   (*d*) commuter engineer.

Explain your answer. _____

_____

10. The author's purpose in writing this selection is to   (*a*) persuade people not to ride trains   (*b*) give information about a train accident (*c*) describe new safety devices on trains   (*d*) suggest a new law.

C. Study Skills

1. Outline the selection in the following format with information from the selection.

   I. The events in the selection
     A. Two trains collided

     B. _____

     C. _____

     D. _____
     E. An investigation is underway

2. Write one complete sentence summarizing the time of day, the site, and the season of the year in which the selection takes place.

_____

_____

D. Writing Skills

1. The selection ends with this sentence: **A full investigation is underway.** In your own words, write a different ending for the selection. You can write one sentence or several sentences.

_____

_____

_____

_____

2. Write one four- to seven-sentence paragraph that includes some of the facts to be investigated about what happened before the accident, during the accident, and after the accident.

_____

_____

_____

_____

 SELECTION C

The five old warriors speak softly of war and American history. They have come from around the country to spend a few days at a Florida hotel. They have come to talk about the past.

More than fifty years ago, these five men stood and crawled and fought and survived together. They were young, foolish, brave, and afraid. They were United States marines—three privates and two corporals.

On April 1, 1945, they came ashore on the island of Okinawa, Japan. The United States Marine Corps, Army, and Navy launched a battle that lasted eighty-two days. It was one of the bloodiest and most important battles of World War II. Amid fire, shrapnel, and bullets, the five marines fought shoulder to shoulder as members of a special unit.

The Japanese call the battle Tennozan, which means "the Final Battle." More than 200,000 Okinawan civilians, 110,000 Japanese soldiers, and 55,000 American servicemen were killed or wounded during the Battle of Okinawa. The Japanese surrendered Okinawa on June 21, 1945, and the war with Japan ended on August 14.

The five marines returned home to quiet, normal lives. But their lives were not quite ordinary. Among them, they have published thirty-three books. They hold thirty-one patents on inventions and a dozen postgraduate college degrees.

On Okinawa in 1945, they thought about the future in minutes, not days—and never months or years. It was enough to stay alive. Now they are in their seventies. They no longer stand as straight as a bayonet or move with youthful ease. But the emotions of this first reunion—and possibly their last—light up the room. They are glad to be together, grateful still to be alive.

PRACTICE THE SKILLS

A. Vocabulary Skills

1. What is **Tennozan**?   (*a*) a Florida hotel   (*b*) an island   (*c*) a battle   (*d*) the title of a book

2. What does the word **launched** mean as it is used in the following sentence? **The United States Marine Corps, Army, and Navy launched a battle that lasted eighty-two days.**   (*a*) began   (*b*) ended   (*c*) won   (*d*) lost

3. What does the word **published** mean as used in the selection?

_____ What is the best context clue word in the sentence that helped you decide your answer?   (*a*) among   (*b*) have   (*c*) thirty-three   (*d*) books

B. Comprehension Skills

1. When did these five men come ashore on the island of Okinawa?

_____

Copy the information to support your answer. _____

_____

2. What was the total number of all people who were killed or wounded in the Battle of Okinawa? (*a*) about 350,000 (*b*) about 200,000 (*c*) about 110,000 (*d*) about 55,000

3. Which of the following events did NOT happen to the five men since World War II? (*a*) They were educated. (*b*) They held a reunion. (*c*) They moved to Florida. (*d*) They wrote books.

4. The major topic for the minor topics **fire, shrapnel, bullets** is (*a*) types of patents (*b*) things in battle (*c*) things soldiers carry (*d*) types of battlefields.

5. Which of the following sets of words best relates to the main idea of the entire selection? (*a*) Okinawa, Japan, Tennozan (*b*) young, foolish, soldiers (*c*) Florida, fifty years, 1945 (*d*) books, patents, degrees

6. How would you best compare the five men in the selection? (*a*) They live near one another. (*b*) They have similar jobs. (*c*) They were marines. (*d*) They were all wounded.

7. The following sentence is an opinion. **They were young, foolish, brave, and afraid.** Copy a fact about the men from the selection.

_____

_____

8. When did the Final Battle end? (*a*) April 1945 (*b*) June 1945 (*c*) March 1970 (*d*) May 1995

9. One of the reasons why these five men survived the Final Battle was that they were (*a*) well trained and lucky (*b*) on boats offshore (*c*) a special reunion group (*d*) graduates of a military college.

10. The author seems to show the most bias in the area of (*a*) countries that win wars (*b*) people who appreciate American history (*c*) people who succeed in life despite difficulties (*d*) government support for veterans.

C. Study Skills

1. Complete the following outline with information from the selection.

    I. People killed or injured in the Final Battle
       A. 200,000 Okinawan civilians

       B. _____

       C. _____

   II. _____
       A. Published thirty-three books
       B. Hold thirty-one patents

       C. _____

2. Summarize in one sentence why the men are getting together for a reunion.

_____

_____

D. Writing Skills

1. Express the idea of this sentence in your own words: **But the emotions of this first reunion—and possibly their last—light up the room.** _____

_____

2. Imagine that you are one of the five ex-marines. About a month BEFORE the reunion, write a letter to one of the others who will attend the reunion. Write at least four sentences.

_____

_____

_____

_____

Unit Activities

Reread each selection carefully and then complete the following activities independently or in cooperative groups.

Connecting the Theme and Selections

1. **Know.** Identify the survival event and where it took place in each selection. Use the following format.

   Survival in Selection A involves a snakebite in a garage.

   Survival in Selection B involves _____

   Survival in Selection C involves _____

2. **Comprehend.** Identify which of the three selections you think most required a combination of luck and skill in order to survive and answer in a few sentences. Introduce your answers with the following: **I think that the events in Selection ___ required the**

   most luck and skill to survive because _____

   _____

   _____

   _____

3. **Apply.** Record a thirty-second introduction of one of the selections for the evening news on radio or television using the word *survival* a few times.

4. **Analyze.** Create one good interview question for a survivor in each selection. Use the following format. Include the word *survive* as often as possible in your questions.

   Selection A. Where did you learn about first aid to survive a snakebite?

   Selection B. _____

   Selection C. _____

5. **Synthesize.** Compose a short song or poem about the theme of survival as it relates to one of the selections. Try to have some rhyming with the word *survive* or *survival.*

6. **Evaluate.** Write a short one- or two-paragraph editorial about one of the selections. Give specific facts and opinions related to how or why the events relating to survival should or could have been avoided. Include the word *survive* or *survival* several times.

Applying the Theme and Selections to the Real World

Use a variety of newspapers, magazines, and other reference materials to complete your choice of the following projects or those assigned to you. Also consider using CD-ROM encyclopedias and other on-line databases as well as television programs and videos to get information for your projects.

Interdisciplinary Project 1

Watch the news on television and read the newspapers for five days. Take notes on about twenty events related to the theme of survival. At the end of the five days, rate the events from 1 to 20 with 1 being the event that you think was the most difficult to survive. Write a short description of each event, including who was involved, what happened, where it happened, why it happened, and how survival related to the event.

Interdisciplinary Project 2

Research World War II in books or interview a World War II veteran about one other famous battle. Summarize the battle in two four- to seven-sentence paragraphs. Include the 5W's of **who** was involved, **what** happened, **where** it took place, **when** it took place, and **why** it took place in the first paragraph. Include the number of lives lost and how the battle affected the outcome of World War II in the second paragraph.

311

Interdisciplinary Project 3

Choose a favorite movie with the theme of survival. Explain the theme with specific information from the movie in two, four- to seven-sentence paragraphs.

Interdisciplinary Project 4

Write a short Survival Manual for an event such as a fire, hurricane, or car accident. Give five to seven organized steps in order to increase the possibility of survival.

Interdisciplinary Project 5

Create a portfolio of three to five drawings showing the theme of survival in different settings. Include a cover page for your portfolio.

UNIT 15

The Theme of
TRADITION

TRADITIONS are customs we celebrate regularly.

PREREADING ACTIVITY

1. Think about all of the examples of tradition that Americans observe or practice.

   a. The annual July Fourth fireworks display
   b. The prom and graduation ceremonies that celebrate the end of high school
   c. A neighborhood block party or cleanup every summer

2. Think about what those traditions celebrate and why they are important to continue.

   a. The birthday of our country and a reminder each year of our rich history
   b. The friendships and hard work that are part of high school and the need to have underclassmen look forward to continuing such a tradition
   c. A time for neighbors to get together and greet new neighbors or to keep their neighborhood clean and appealing

3. Now give two examples of your own for tradition, and explain why that tradition is important to continue.

A first example is done for you.

Example 1. The Olympic torch is lighted at the Summer and Winter Games every two years to celebrate the beginning of the two-week event.

Example 2. _____

_____

Example 3. _____

_____

SELECTION A

Check the box score for any baseball game. It shows the number of runs, hits, and errors for each team. In this story, one high school's baseball team made hits and runs—and one great big error.

For thirty-four years, Jefferson High and Barnstead High have been baseball rivals. It's an annual tradition. Each year the two schools' teams play a heated game. They battle on the baseball diamond for bragging rights as the best team in their region of the state.

For the past twelve years, Jefferson's baseball team had a quiet tradition only they knew about. It caused them a lot of trouble this year.

Jefferson's varsity baseball team had just won a thrilling come-from-behind, last-inning victory. The thirty players and their coach had an hour's ride home on the bus. Every year, as they had done for the past twelve years, the driver stopped at the same convenience store. All of the players streamed off the bus and into the store. Within several minutes, they were back on the bus, headed for home. But while they were in the store, they had a shoplifting spree. Candy, gum, soda, potato chips, and other snacks moved into their backpacks and pockets with precision and speed. More than $100 worth of merchandise was pilfered. This was probably much more than the total of what they paid for.

This year, however, there was a witness. Kim Anderson, the store manager, observed the shoplifting scene on the closed-circuit TV in her office. Anderson endured a very sleepless night. The next morning she brought the video to Jefferson's principal. At noon, everyone on the baseball team viewed the tape.

Later that afternoon, the entire team showed up in the athletic director's office. Each player had his uniform in his hand. Nearly all of the players confessed to shoplifting at the convenience store.

The team paid a steep price for the stolen candy and potato chips. Jefferson forfeited the remaining seven games in the season. Both varsity and junior varsity games were canceled, including the Barnstead thriller. It would be a long off-season wait before the next Jefferson High baseball game. And there were revisions to the code of conduct in the school's handbook.

PRACTICE THE SKILLS

A. Vocabulary Skills

1. The word **annual** means   (a) daily   (b) weekly   (c) monthly   (d) yearly.

Use the word in a sentence of your own. _____

_____

2. The word **streamed** as it is used in the selection refers to (a) swam in a river   (b) stood in line   (c) sat still   (d) move quickly.

3. In the phrase **nearly all of the players confessed to participating,** the word **confessed** could be replaced with (a) denied   (b) admitted   (c) volunteered   (d) blamed.

B. Comprehension Skills

1. Copy one sentence from the selection that contains the best information to answer the question, **What proof did Kim Anderson have to support the shoplifting charges?** _____

_____

2. How many years had the shoplifting tradition been happening? (a) seven   (b) twelve   (c) thirty-four   (d) thirty-five

317

3. What event happened after the team viewed the tape?   (*a*) It was given to the school administration.   (*b*) The shoplifting occurred. (*c*) The team showed up in the athletic director's office.   (*d*) The team got back on the bus.

4. The major topic about the selection for the minor topics **candy, gum, soda, chips** is _____

5. The best main idea for the selection is
   (*a*) Baseball team wins a game but loses the season
   (*b*) Baseball team wins thriller in last inning
   (*c*) Baseball team punished too heavily for shoplifting
   (*d*) Jefferson and Barnstead High baseball tradition ends

6. What was the direct cause of the team's forfeiting seven games? (*a*) Kim Anderson and the videotape   (*b*) the traditional rivalry with Barnstead   (*c*) disagreement between the coach and the players (*d*) the team's unsportsmanlike conduct during the game

7. Copy one sentence from the selection that states a fact.

   _____

   _____

   Copy one sentence that is an opinion. _____

   _____

8. Do you think that the coach of Jefferson High knew about the shoplifting tradition? Why or why not? _____

   _____

9. Why did Kim Anderson endure **a very sleepless night** according to the selection? _____

   _____

TRADITION

10. The author's main purpose in writing this selection is to show (*a*) the value of high school sports (*b*) how high school sports can cause injuries (*c*) how rules can be broken (*d*) how some traditions are not good.

C. Study Skills

1. Complete the following outline with information from the selection.

    1. Some major events leading up to the end of the Jefferson baseball season

       A. The team defeated Barnstead High

       B. _____

       C. _____

       D. _____

       E. _____

2. Complete the following sentence. **If I were Kim Anderson, I would/would not have given the tape to school officials**

because _____

_____

_____

D. Writing Skills

1. Write two sentences that tell how the whole shoplifting incident could have been avoided.

_____

_____

_____

319

2. Write a newspaper article of at least four sentences telling about the tradition in this selection. Include information about the 5W's of who, what happened, where, when, and why. _____

_____

_____

_____

_____

 SELECTION B

My choice for the number-one holiday of the year is Thanksgiving. It's a truly American holiday, one with a long tradition.

The first Thanksgiving was celebrated in 1621. The governor of Plymouth Colony declared a day of thanksgiving to celebrate the colonists' first harvest. The Pilgrims and their Indian neighbors sat down together to a feast of corn and wild turkey. In 1789, after the American Revolution, President George Washington declared the first national Thanksgiving Day.

Thanksgiving has endured more than 350 years without becoming an overly commercialized holiday. Except for a few big-city parades and high school football games, Thanksgiving Day is reserved and preserved for family get-togethers.

When I was young, I remember that the men sat in the living room and tried to solve the problems of the world. The women owned the kitchen. They prepared the feast, served the meal, and cleaned up all the mess. Now the transition has gone full circle. On Turkey Day, I find myself affectionately referred to as the Old Bird, Mr. Tom, and the Pie Man. My male friends assume similar roles as chief cook and cleanup person.

At each Thanksgiving dinner, I look around the table

and stop to think how much I appreciate those old faces among family and friends. Each year we add a few new faces, too.

Thanksgiving in our house is still a day for debate and world problem solving. But now there is equal participation across age and gender. Everyone joins the debate. There are never any winners or losers, though. Our discussions always end in a draw.

In our house and across the country, Thanksgiving is a day to toast the good life. It is a time to be thankful for family and friends, a time to appreciate all that we have. We look forward each year to this American tradition that seems to get better with age.

PRACTICE THE SKILLS

A. Vocabulary Skills

1. The best example of **an overly commercialized holiday** is (*a*) Christmas   (*b*) Halloween   (*c*) Fourth of July   (*d*) Thanksgiving.

2. The best word to take the place of **affectionately** as used in the selection is   (*a*) respectfully   (*b*) fondly   (*c*) discouragingly (*d*) rarely.

3. **Debate** as used in the selection refers to   (*a*) eating   (*b*) talking (*c*) carving   (*d*) cooking.

B. Comprehension Skills

1. Copy the sentence that gives the reason why we celebrate Thanksgiving Day.

_____

_____

2. Which of the following events occur most on Thanksgiving Day?
(*a*) Native American festivals (*b*) parades (*c*) baseball games
(*d*) TV debates

3. The author says that what has changed most about Thanksgiving
since he was a young boy is (*a*) the food (*b*) the roles of men and
women (*c*) the purpose of the holiday (*d*) the football games.

4. Name the three minor topics from the selection for the major topic

Thanksgiving Day foods. _____

_____

_____

5. Choose the title that you think best summarizes the selection's main
idea. (*a*) Family Debates (*b*) National Holidays (*c*) Thanksgiving
Traditions (*d*) Thanksgiving Foods

6. Tell one way the first Thanksgiving Day was like Thanksgiving today.

_____

Tell one way the first Thanksgiving was different from Thanksgiving

today. _____

_____

7. The words **We, seems,** and **better** all indicate that the last sentence
is an opinion. Write one sentence from the selection that you are
sure is a fact.

_____

_____

8. The author or narrator is referred to as **the Old Bird, Mr. Tom,
and the Pie Man.** Which of the following groups of people do you
think uses these nicknames the most? More than one choice may be
possible, depending on your opinion. (*a*) neighbors (*b*) coworkers
(*c*) friends (*d*) family members

9. You would think that Thanksgiving Day is special because it (*a*) brings family together   (*b*) provides added profits for stores (*c*) provides the best meal of the year   (*d*) allows world problems to be solved.

10. What word do you think best describes the author's feeling about Thanksgiving Day?   (*a*) toleration   (*b*) spiritual   (*c*) appreciation (*d*) concern

C. Study Skills

1. Complete the following outline with information from the selection and information of your own.

    I. Four reasons why Thanksgiving is an American tradition
       A. Celebrates the events of 1621

       B. _____

       C. _____

       D. _____

2. In the last paragraph, what do you think the author means by **the good life**? Give some examples. Write two or three sentences.

_____

_____

D. Writing Skills

1. Stop and think for a minute. What are you thankful for? Write two or three sentences.

_____

_____

_____

2. Write at least four sentences that give your opinions about the following. **My choice for number-one holiday is** _____

_____

_____

_____

_____

_____

 ## SELECTION C

Sometime between the California Gold Rush of 1849 and the beginning of the Civil War in 1861, John Alden Conwell started his one-man company. The John Alden Conwell Trading Company began in a little town outside of Philadelphia. Conwell was a craftsman. He worked with hides from cattle, pigs, and deer. From these hides, he made clothing and leather goods such as shoes, saddles, handbags, and gloves.

Today the JAC Trading Company is a multimillion-dollar family tradition. Some 150 years have passed, and five generations of Conwells have headed the company over the years.

John A. Conwell, Jr., was the founder's son. He introduced mass production when he hired ten apprentices. They learned to produce the same quality goods that he and his father made. Now the Trading Company had more goods to sell.

Next came John A., the third, who led the company into the twentieth century. During his time as chairman, the automobile was invented. When the company won a contract to produce leather seats in new cars, more employees and more production space were added. World War I brought the company profitable government contracts. New employees were hired to produce clothing and backpacks for soldiers.

During the postwar 1920s and 1930s, there was a surge in new styles of clothing and women's fashions. In the late 1930s, John A., the fourth, began catalog sales and chain store sales. The company won sizable government contracts for military supplies during World War II.

The postwar boom in the American economy through the 1980s brought the company to fifty years of unprecedented growth and success. The JAC Trading Company became one of the most successful businesses in America. The key to its success was increased emphasis on quality clothing and goods made of cotton, denim, and the new synthetic materials, such as nylon and rayon. In 1989, the company went public and sold shares of stock to investors. On the New York Stock Exchange, its reference letters were JAC—of course.

This happened just in time for the eighty-eight-year-old, John A., the fourth, to hand the reins of control to his granddaughter, Jacquelyn (Jackie) Alden Conwell-Atkins. The tradition of a family CEO (chief executive officer) continued. But in the twenty-first century, management would be in the hands of a woman for the first time. Another Conwell descendant had worked her way to the top.

In the twenty-first century, the economy will be global, so JAC's new management will look for new markets abroad. JAC will focus on customer satisfaction and quality designer products at competitive prices. Jackie, the new CEO, hopes to expand sales through use of the Internet and cable TV home shopping. Her vision also includes school and community partnerships and scholarship programs for business students.

New goals and challenges lie ahead for the multi-million-dollar JAC Trading Company. This huge company continues its tradition of hard work and quality products that began long ago with a one-man shop in a little town near Philadelphia.

TRADITION

PRACTICE THE SKILLS
☑

A. Vocabulary Skills

1. Descendants are   (*a*) companies   (*b*) clothing   (*c*) people
(*d*) traditions.

Use **descendants** in a sentence of your own _____

_____

2. The word **surge** as used in the phrase **a surge in new styles of clothing** means   (*a*) increase   (*b*) decrease   (*c*) end   (*d*) beginning.

3. In the phrase **fifty years of unprecedented growth,** the word **unprecedented** means   (*a*) never to happen again   (*b*) never before
(*c*) without cost   (*d*) without leadership.

B. Comprehension Skills

1. Facts about the contributions of John Alden Conwell, the fourth, can be found mostly in which paragraphs?   (*a*) first and second
(*b*) second and third   (*c*) fourth and fifth   (*d*) fifth and sixth

2. The best word to describe the founder of the JAC Trading Company is   (*a*) craftsman   (*b*) businessman   (*c*) salesman   (*d*) apprentice.

3. What event occurred just after the company went public on the New York Stock Exchange?   (*a*) Catalog and chain store sales expanded.
(*b*) Denim was used in many products.   (*c*) Jacquelyn Alden Conwell-Atkins took over.   (*d*) None of these.

4. The major topic for the minor topics **new markets, customer satisfaction, use of the Internet, school partnerships** is
(*a*) goals from 1850 to 1900   (*b*) goals from 1900 to 1950   (*c*) goals from 1950 to 1989   (*d*) goals of the twenty-first century.

5. Write a one-sentence main idea of your own for the entire selection.

_____

_____

6. In the years from 1914 to 1945, one of the company's major sources of income was   (*a*) the sale of stock   (*b*) government contracts for military supplies   (*c*) sales on the Internet and cable TV (*d*) scholarship programs for business students.

7. Copy one fact about one of the five Conwells. Then rewrite it into an opinion.

Fact. _____

Opinion. _____

8. The selection doesn't explain why eighty-eight-year-old John A., the fourth, turned over the company to his granddaughter instead of to one of his sons or daughters. Think of two reasons that might explain his action.

_____

_____

9. How would you describe the financial condition of the company as it enters the twenty-first century?   (*a*) excellent   (*b*) good   (*c*) fair (*d*) poor

Give one reason for your answer. _____

_____

10. Which one of the Conwell family members do you think made (or will make) the most important contribution to the John Alden

Conwell Trading Company? _____

Explain the reason for your choice. _____

_____

_____

C. Study Skills

1. Complete the following outline with information from the selection.

    I. The history of the Conwell family and the major contributions of each
      A. John Alden Conwell
        1. Started the company in the mid-1850s
        2. Made things out of animal hides

      B. _____

        1. _____

        2. _____

      C. _____

        1. _____

        2. _____

      D. _____

        1. _____

        2. _____
      E. Jacquelyn Alden Conwell-Atkins

        1. _____

        2. _____

   II. Five traditions for success in the JAC Trading Company
        1. Work hard

        2. _____

        3. _____

        4. _____
        5. Plan for the future

2. Choose one important event in the history of the company. Summarize in one sentence why you think it was important to the success of the company. _____

_____

_____

D. Writing Skills

1. Write one sentence giving two reasons why you think Jackie will be successful. _____

_____

Now write one sentence giving two problems that she might have.

_____

2. You are a stockbroker recommending stocks to buy for your customers. Write at least four sentences explaining why JAC Trading Company is a good investment.

_____

_____

_____

_____

_____

Unit Activities

Reread each selection carefully and then complete the following activities independently or in cooperative groups.

TRADITION

Connecting the Theme and Selections

1. **Know.** Recall the major tradition and one minor tradition from each selection.

   Example. In Selection A, the major tradition is the annual baseball game and the minor tradition is the shoplifting.

   In Selection B, _____

   _____

   In Selection C, _____

   _____

2. **Comprehend.** Identify which selection shows what you think is the most important tradition and give three reasons for your choice. Use the following format.

   Selection _____ represents the most important tradition.

   Reason 1. _____

   Reason 2. _____

   Reason 3. _____

3. **Apply.** Illustrate with your own three drawings the ending of one tradition from each selection. One example for each selection follows.

   In Selection A, the team admits to shoplifting and hands in their uniforms.
   In Selection B, fewer women and more men cook on Thanksgiving Day.
   In Selection C, Jacquelyn A. Conwell-Atkins is the first woman to lead the company.

4. **Analyze.** List one reason why you think the major tradition continues in each selection. Use the following format.

   The baseball rivalry tradition continues in Selection A because

   _____

   _____

The Thanksgiving holiday tradition continues in Selection B because

_____

The JAC Trading Company tradition continues in Selection C

because _____

_____

5. **Synthesize.** Compose a poem or song about tradition by referring to all three selections.

6. **Evaluate.** Predict one new tradition for each selection in the years ahead and explain how that tradition will improve the topic of each selection.

Selection A. _____

Selection B. _____

Selection C. _____

Applying the Theme and Selections to the Real World

Use a variety of newspapers, magazines, and other reference materials to complete your choice of the following projects or those assigned to you. Also consider using CD-ROM encyclopedias and other on-line databases as well as television programs and videos to get information for your projects.

Interdisciplinary Project 1

Review the Code of Conduct for your school. Create a report about some of the rules associated with conduct and school sports. Also describe any school rules associated with hazing and why school hazing rules and state hazing laws exist.

Interdisciplinary Project 2

Create a collage of ten traditions. Include two for each of the following categories: sports, holidays, business, family, and school.

Interdisciplinary Project 3

Research one holiday observed in other countries. Write report about this holiday and include at least three traditions about it.

Interdisciplinary Project 4

Research the story and play *Fiddler on the Roof.* Explain the lyrics in the song "Tradition" and how the traditions are about the meaning of the story.

Interdisciplinary Project 5

Invent a new American holiday. Give it a name, a date, reasons for observing it, and at least two traditions associated with it. Complete your answers in report form.

UNIT 16

The Theme of
WORK

Definition

WORK is the effort needed to accomplish or produce something. Work is what you do for employment. It is a duty or a task.

PREREADING ACTIVITY

1. Think about several examples of work that you see other people do every day and the reasons why people work.

   a. People building houses
   b. People delivering the news on television
   c. People performing medical surgery

2. Think of the preparation and training that go into each of these examples of work.

   a. Apprentice courses in vocational education
   b. Going to college to study television journalism
   c. Going to medical school for many years and then practicing in a hospital

3. Now give three examples of your own of work that you do or see other people doing and the reason for the work. An example is provided.

A first example is done for you.

Example. A basketball player practices or plays in a game to defeat the opponent.

Example. _____

_____

Example. _____

_____

Example. _____

_____

SELECTION A

Arthur Yee Chin died recently at the age of eighty-one. Mr. Chin, a businessman, was born in China. At the age of eight, he immigrated alone to the United States. Three uncles in America paid for his thirty-day voyage on a freighter. By the time he was fourteen, Mr. Chin owned and operated a laundry. He had learned the laundry business by working for one of his uncles. Some years later, he opened a successful Chinese restaurant.

Mr. Chin's aunt died when he was only nine. He became like a mother to his three cousins. He would wake them, feed them breakfast, and get them off to school. This would make him late to school, so as a punishment he would have to serve detention (stay after school). Because detention made him late for work in his uncle's laundry, his uncle would punish him, too.

When his uncle remarried, Mr. Chin set off on his own and opened his own laundry. He was fourteen years old. After closing the laundry each day, he would pull down the shades and cook his meals on a potbellied stove. Each night he would roll out his board and mattress and sleep on the floor. He balanced his own books and sent some of his profits to his parents in China. He never saw them again after coming to America.

His restaurant was the first drive-in Chinese restaurant in the area. It was popular and successful.

After more than sixty years of working seven days a week and eighteen hours a day, Mr. Arthur Chin finally retired at the age of seventy-five. He spent the last six years doing charity work in his community. He spent his winters in Florida, mostly fishing and relaxing.

PRACTICE THE SKILLS

A. Vocabulary Skills

1. The word **immigrated** as used in the selection means   (a) to come
(b) to leave   (c) to die   (d) to marry.

2. A **freighter** is probably   (a) a truck   (b) a car   (c) an airplane
(d) a ship.

   Explain how you came up with your answer by referring to context

   clues in the sentence. _____

   _____

3. The word **balanced** as used in the phrase **balanced his own books**
has a meaning most related to   (a) an athlete   (b) a teacher   (c) a
banker   (d) a doctor.

   Explain your answer by referring to the context clue **profits** in the
sentence.

   _____

   _____

B. Comprehension Skills

1. Copy the sentence that gives the information about how often Mr.

   Chin saw his parents after coming to America. _____

   _____

2. How old was Mr. Chin when his aunt died?   (a) eight   (b) nine
(c) fourteen   (d) seventy-five

337

WORK

3. What would Mr. Chin do after closing his own laundry each day? (*a*) pull down the shades and cook his meals (*b*) feed his cousins breakfast and get them off to school (*c*) go to school (*d*) do charity work and go fishing

4. The best major topic for the minor topics **laundry** and **restaurant** is (*a*) places where Mr. Chin's cousins worked (*b*) failing businesses in China (*c*) types of businesses owned by Mr. Chin (*d*) types of businesses Mr. Chin opened in Florida.

5. Choose the sentence that best expresses the main idea of the selection:
(*a*) Immigrating to America is hard for a young child.
(*b*) Mr. Chin's uncle treated him badly.
(*c*) Mr. Chin worked hard, starting at a young age, and was successful.
(*d*) Even when he retired, Mr. Chin was forced to work.

6. What was the cause of Mr. Chin's tardiness at school? _____

_____

What was the effect? _____

_____

7. Review the sentences that contain numbers. Most of those sentences are (*a*) facts (*b*) opinions (*c*) a balance of facts and opinions.

Explain your answer. _____

_____

8. Describe Mr. Chin's financial condition when he retired. _____

_____

9. Why do you think Mr. Chin set off on his own after his uncle remarried? (*a*) He was ready to start his own business. (*b*) He didn't want to be a burden for his uncle with a new wife. (*c*) His cousins were older. (*d*) All of these.

10. Which word best describes the author's attitude toward Mr. Chin? (*a*) dislike   (*b*) jealousy   (*c*) respect   (*d*) fondness

Explain your answer in one sentence. _____

_____

C. Study Skills

1. Complete the following outline of major events in Mr. Chin's life.

    I. Mr. Chin's lifetime
      A. Came to America at eight

      B. _____

      C. _____

      D. _____

      E. _____
      F. Died at eighty-one

2. Summarize what kind of person Mr. Chin was in one sentence of your own. Use at least two or three different words to describe him.

_____

D. Writing Skills

1. Imagine what Mr. Chin thought and felt during his younger years. Write a diary entry that he might have written when he was eight, nine, or fourteen.

_____

_____

_____

_____

_____

2. Write a sample letter that Mr. Chin wrote to his parents when sending money back to them in China. Include at least four

sentences. _____

_____

_____

_____

_____

 SELECTION B

What is the most demanding athletic event? Few people would disagree that it's the triathlon. A triathlon is a single event that includes swimming, bicycling, and running. Triathletes (athletes who compete in a triathlon) do not stop between these three events.

A triathlon starts with a 2.4-mile swim. Immediately after the swim, triathletes jump onto their bikes for a 112-mile bike race. At the finish line, they hop off their bikes and run 26.2 miles. Then they can stop. The entire event usually consists of eight or nine hours of grueling competition.

A triathlete's body and mind must be perfectly prepared for race day. Training can take as much as ten years before the body is ready. A typical training week for the serious triathlete involves six days of training. Each training day is six to eight hours long. A triathlete in training usually swims, runs, and bikes eighteen to twenty times a week. There are also five or six strength sessions.

Diet is important, too. The triathlete eats three thousand to six thousand calories a day to keep going. Most people would get very fat on such a diet, but triathletes burn off all those extra calories.

The triathlon has a certain mystique to it. Both women and men compete in the event. The success of these "ironmen" and "ironwomen" is usually tied to their attitude.

Some are very disciplined in their training. Others are very serious and focused. Still others are laid back. Whatever the athlete's attitude, competing in a triathlon is one long commitment and a whole lot of work on race day.

PRACTICE THE SKILLS

A. Vocabulary Skills

1. You would assume that the words **triathlete** and **triathlon** each have something to do with the number   (a) 1   (b) 3   (c) 2   (d) 112.

   Explain your answer. _____

   _____

2. In the phrase **eight or nine hours of grueling competition,** the word **grueling** is best replaced by the words   (a) somewhat difficult   (b) extremely difficult   (c) somewhat easy   (d) extremely easy.

3. Rewrite the following sentence into your own words. **The triathlon has a certain mystique to it.** _____

   _____

B. Comprehension Skills

1. The paragraph that gives the most detailed information about the triathlon's events is   (a) first   (b) second   (c) fourth   (d) fifth.

2. How many days a week does the average triathlete train?   (a) four   (b) five   (c) six   (d) seven

3. What is the sequence of events in a triathlon?   (a) bike, run, swim   (b) swim, run, bike   (c) run, bike, swim   (d) swim, bike, run

4. Give three minor topics from the selection for the major topic **things a triathlete in training does.** _____

_____

_____

5. Use the following words to write a one-sentence main idea of your own for the entire selection: **triathlon, event, training, competition.** _____

_____

_____

6. According to the selection, what different attitudes do triathletes have toward their training? Write at least three sentences.

_____

_____

_____

7. Rewrite the following fact into an opinion. **The triathlete eats three thousand to six thousand calories a day.** _____

_____

8. According to the selection, the three factors that contribute most to a triathlete's success are   (*a*) training, diet, attitude   (*b*) previous victories, strength, weight   (*c*) youth, attitude, height   (*d*) age, previous victories, weather.

9. You would reason that the least one must do on race day is (*a*) have the fastest time in one event   (*b*) complete the three events in less than six hours   (*c*) complete all three events   (*d*) eat three thousand to six thousand calories for breakfast. Explain your

answer. _____

_____

10. What is the author's purpose in writing this selection?　(*a*) to get you to compete in a triathlon　(*b*) to inform you about the demands of the triathlon　(*c*) to describe the results of a triathlon　(*d*) to introduce you to the world's best triathlete

C.　Study Skills

1. Complete the following outline using information from the selection.

    I. Events in the triathlon
      A. 2.4-mile swim

      B. _____

      C. _____

   II. _____
      A. six days a week
      B. six to eight hours a day

      C. _____

      D. _____

2. Summarize which one of the three triathlon events you think is the most difficult and explain your reasons in a few sentences.

_____

_____

_____

D.　Writing Skills

1. Imagine that you are a triathlete. You are competing in a triathlon tomorrow. What three things would you do the night before the event? Write two or three sentences.

_____

_____

_____

2. Think about sports other than the triathlon. Finish this sentence: **The athlete I most admire is** _____. Now think of three reasons why you admire that athlete. Write each reason in a separate sentence.

_____

_____

_____

Write a paragraph that starts with a topic sentence (your opinion). Your paragraph should have three more sentences (your supporting reasons).

_____

_____

_____

_____

_____

_____

 SELECTION C

Up in central Vermont there's a town nicknamed "Mud City." In Vermont, every season brings its own unique beauty. In spring, the snow melts and trees bud. On the maple trees, sap is collected in buckets. The sap will become Vermont's famous maple syrup, destined to be poured over pancakes and waffles. In summer, the trees and grass are lush green. Vermont's fall foliage is spectacular. Cars filled with "leaf-peekers" cause traffic jams as they admire the trees' brilliant colors. Winter brings bone-biting cold and snow—and skiers.

Through all seasons and all weathers, farms need constant tending. Cows need daily milking.

WORK

This is a story about three special sisters—Gertrude, Jeanette, and Therese. They were born on a farm near Mud City and grew up there. Each left soon after high school graduation. They were bound for college and careers. Gertrude became a teacher. Jeanette flew as a flight attendant. Therese worked in Washington, D.C., as secretary to a Vermont senator.

When they were in their thirties, all three sisters made an important decision. Separately, they each decided to come back to work the family farm. The farm had 670 acres and a herd of Jersey cows. Gertrude, the teacher, returned to the farm in 1952. Jeanette came home in 1957 and Therese a year later.

Their father died in 1957. Their mother died in 1995. She had continued working the farm until she was ninety.

Recently, a local newspaper wrote about the three sisters. They felt guilty, the story said, about leaving the milking business at the ages of sixty-six, sixty-eight, and seventy-one. They will continue to live in the farmhouse together. Their herd of dairy cows will soon be auctioned. The land has already been sold to the state government, which wants to preserve farmland.

Soon the sisters will have no more 3:30 A.M. milking calls. No more evening doses of aspirin for aches and pains. No more falling asleep right after dinner with a book in hand. These three unique ladies will enjoy a little rest after a lifetime of labors that they loved.

PRACTICE THE SKILLS

A. Vocabulary Skills

1. In the phrase **Vermont's fall foliage is spectacular,** what does **foliage** mean? (Hint: Look at the context for clues.)   (*a*) weather (*b*) sap from trees   (*c*) leaves of trees   (*d*) cultural and sports events

2. In the phrase **farms need constant tending,** the word **tending** could be replaced with any of the following EXCEPT   (*a*) repair   (*b*) weather   (*c*) attention   (*d*) care.

3. The word **unique** is used twice in the selection. A word from the selection that could replace **unique** is   (*a*) constant   (*b*) tender   (*c*) little   (*d*) special.

B. Comprehension Skills

1. Which paragraph contains the answer to the question, **What careers did the three sisters enter after college graduation?**   (*a*) first   (*b*) second   (*c*) third   (*d*) fourth

2. How many acres was the farm?   (*a*) 71   (*b*) 90   (*c*) none of these

3. After the father died, what was the sequence of the three sisters returning to the farm?   (*a*) Therese, Jeanette, Gertrude   (*b*) Gertrude, Jeanette, Therese   (*c*) Jeanette, Gertrude, Therese   (*d*) Therese, Gertrude, Jeanette

4. What is the major topic for the minor topics **sapping maple trees, summer green, fall foliage, winter days**? _____

5. Write a main idea sentence of your own about the entire selection. Include the word *work*. _____

_____

6. Which of the following statements is NOT true about all three sisters?   (*a*) They left the farm after they graduated from high school.   (*b*) They had careers.   (*c*) They returned to the farm the same year.   (*d*) They retired together.

7. How would you describe the selection?   (*a*) mostly facts   (*b*) mostly opinions   (*c*) about the same number of facts as opinions. Explain your answer. _____

_____

_____

8. You would infer that the healthiest member of the entire family was (a) the father   (b) the mother   (c) Gertrude   (d) Jeanette. Explain

your answer. _____

_____

_____

9. You would reason that the three sisters had no problem selling the farm to the government because of   (a) the quality of the land   (b) the value of the cows   (c) Therese's career and contacts   (d) the need to build a school.

10. The author's main purpose is to   (a) give detailed information about dairy farming   (b) persuade readers to move to Vermont   (c) describe the lives of three hard-working women   (d) discuss some of the problems of retirement.

C. Study Skills

1. Complete the following outline by using information from the selection.

    I. Important events in the lives of the three sisters
      A. The sisters were born on the farm

      B. _____

      C. _____

      D. _____

      E. _____
      F. The sisters retired

2. Summarize in two sentences the average workday in the lives of the

three sisters. _____

_____

_____

D. Writing Skills

1. Why do you think the sisters retired? Give at least two goods reasons in one well-written sentence. _____

_____

2. You are a local newspaper or TV reporter. Write a paragraph about the retirement of the three sisters. Write at least four sentences.

_____

_____

_____

_____

_____

Unit Activities

Reread each selection carefully and then complete the following activities independently or in small groups.

Connecting the Theme and Selections

1. **Know.** List the main person(s) from each selection and the main type(s) of work each did. Use the following format.

The main person in Selection A was Mr. Chin. He owned a laundry and a restaurant.

The main person(s) _____

_____

The main person(s) _____

_____

2. Comprehend. List the three selections in order of least difficult work to most difficult work, followed by one reason for your answer. Use the following format.

Selection _____ was the least difficult work because _____

Selection _____ was the next most difficult work because _____

Selection _____ was the most difficult work because _____

3. Apply. Prepare an interview with one of the main persons in the selection that you think showed the most difficult work. Write three questions that you would ask that person.

4. Analyze. Survey five people using the format in Comprehend above. Summarize the three selections for each person, then ask his or her opinions of least difficult, next most difficult, and most difficult. Create a graph of their answers.

5. Synthesize. Pretend that you are to present an award to the main person(s) in each selection. Write two to three sentences that you would say about each before you called him or her to accept the award.

6. Evaluate. Decide which of the three selections showed people involved in the theme of work that most affects other people. Give several reasons to support your answer in at least four sentences. Introduce your paragraph with the following topic sentence.

I think that Selection _____ showed a person whose work most affects other people.

Applying the Theme and Selections to the Real World

Use a variety of newspapers, magazines, and other reference materials to complete your choice of the following projects or those assigned to you. Also consider using CD-ROM encyclopedias and other on-line databases as well as television programs and videos to get information for your projects.

WORK

Interdisciplinary Project 1

Create a chart of work that shows what many people did for a living in each century of our history. Give two examples and a short description of each for each century. Include pictures, if possible. Consider the following format.

Work in the 1600s

Example 1. _____

Example 2. _____

Work in the 1700s

Example 1. _____

Example 2. _____

Work in the 1800s

Example 1. _____

Example 2. _____

Work in the 1900s

Example 1. _____

Example 2. _____

Work in the 2000s

Example 1. _____

Example 2. _____

Interdisciplinary Project 2

Interview five different friends, relatives, and professionals. Ask each person the following five questions and put your information from each into five paragraphs.
1. What kind of work do you do?

2. What kind of training or preparation did you need for your work?
3. Do you consider your work to be difficult? How or why is it difficult?
4. Do you enjoy your work? Why or why not?
5. If you could do any kind of work, what would it be? Why?

Interdisciplinary Project 3

Create a chart of time, workouts, and diet for an athlete.

Interdisciplinary Project 4

Create a collage of five pictures and/or drawings of your own showing people involved in the theme of work. Include types of work that are more physical and types that involve more thinking. Arrange your pictures and/or drawings from least difficult to most difficult. Include a caption stating conclusions you reached about the theme of work.

Interdisciplinary Project 5

Create a class time capsule. List what each person will be doing for work twenty years from now and one reason for each choice. Put it in a secure place for future reference at an event such as a class reunion.

Answers to
Practice Unit

A. Vocabulary Skills

1. (c)

2. (b)

3. (d)

B. Comprehension Skills

1. (c)

2. (c)

3. (d)

4. (a)

5. (c)

6. (b)

7. Fact 1 example: Mr. Peterson wrote *Field Guide to Birds* in 1934. Fact 2 example: To this point, the book has sold some 8 million copies. Opinion example: *Field Guide to Birds* is the best book ever written about birds.

8. (b)

9. (b)

10. (a)

C. Study Skills

1. Example:
    I. Some facts about Roger Tory Peterson
        A. Died a few years ago at the age of 87
        B. Will be remembered as the Birdman of America
        C. Wrote *Field Guide to Birds* in 1934
    II. Some facts about *Field Guide to Birds*

A. 8 million copies sold
B. Translated into 12 languages
C. Began a new era of appreciation for wildlife
D. Contains information and pictures of 5,000 birds
E. It allows people to identify types of birds in the outdoors

2. Example: Roger Tory Peterson wrote a book about bird-watching and spent his life getting more people interested in the activity.

D. Writing Skills

1. Example: People like to watch birds because it gets them outdoors to appreciate nature.

2. Example: Bird-watching could become a sport. Some of the rules might be to watch a specific number of different birds over a specific amount of time. You would have to use Peterson's book and give the name of the bird and the time and place you saw it. Maybe one out of every three birds watched would have to have an original photograph taken by the bird-watcher.

Answers to Practice Unit

SELECTION C

A. Vocabulary Skills

1. (c)
2. (a)
3. (b)

B. Comprehension Skills

1. Choose one. For many years our ocean boundaries, especially the Georges Bank area of the Atlantic, have been overly fished by both Americans and foreigners. But the once-rich fishing grounds off New England are still not replenishing to meet the demand.

2. (d)

3. (c)

4. (b)

5. Example: The new industry of aquaculture is before us.

6. (a)

7. (b)

8. (c)

9. (d)

10. (b)

C. Study Skills

1. Example:
 I. Problems I learned about in the fishing industry
   A. Overly fished by Americans and foreigners
   B. Trawlers with huge nets dragged millions of tons of fish
   C. No regard for the time it takes to replace these ocean creatures
 II. Government laws and programs I learned about in the fishing industry
   A. Mileage limits
   B. Number of fishing days reduced
   C. Boat buy-back programs
 III. Things I learned about aquaculture
   A. New businesses would purchase parcels of ocean from the government
   B. Cod, haddock, and flounder would be grown
   C. Technology would be used to improve techniques
   D. Fish farms could even become tourist areas
   E. New jobs and quality food will be provided

2. Example: I think that aquaculture will expand because it is a 100 billion dollar business that will provide new jobs and quality food supplies.

D. Writing Skills

1. Example: Aquaculture will expand into the 21st century in the Atlantic Ocean because fish is needed for food.

Example: Because fish is needed for food, aquaculture will expand in the Atlantic Ocean into the 21st century.

2. Example: There will be many good jobs in the aquaculture industry. One good job will be as a biologist using technology to provide feeding schedules for the fish. A second good job will be as a lawyer to write contracts for the businesses to buy the ocean parcels from the government.

Sample Answers or Explanations for Unit Activities

Connecting the Theme and Selections

1. Know

Example:
In Selection A, I learned about studies that show the more you learn in school, the more you earn in your lifetime.
In Selection B, I learned about Roger Tory Peterson, who wrote about bird-watching, and how his book has more people doing this activity.
In Selection C, I learned about the fishing industry and the new business of fish farming called aquaculture.

2. Comprehend

Example:
Selection A has the most effect on the most people because people have to go to school and then have to go to work. The selection tells about how much more money you will earn based on how much more education you have.

3. Apply

Explanation:
Students need to choose one or two pictures that show some kind of job differences and the education and earnings associated with each. Or a picture about bird-watching. Or a picture or two about farming on land and farming in the ocean.

4. Analyze

Example:

Two jobs in the aquaculture industry might be a biologist who researches fish diseases and a tour director who drives the boat to the fish pens and explains how the fish are grown. The biologist will require more training and probably an advanced degree in the science of biology. The tour director will require good speaking and communication skills and maybe a college degree. The biologist will likely earn a lot more money in his/her career than the tour director.

5. Synthesize

Explanation:

A song or poem with a variety of lyrics or a verse about the topic of bird-watching or fish farming is the assignment. A bird-watching topic should include a reference to Roger Tory Peterson and the benefits of bird-watching. A fish-farming topic should include a reference to aquaculture and its benefits. The lyrics or verse may or may not rhyme.

6. Evaluate

Example:

My career or job will be a teacher. I will have to go to college and get at least one degree to start teaching. After, I will probably get an advanced degree. I will earn about 50 thousand dollars a year for my thirty years in the field. This will amount to about one and a half million dollars of lifetime income.